A Sketch

of

English Legal History

By

Frederic W. Maitland, LL.D., D.C.L.

Late Downing Professor of the Laws of England in the University of Cambridge

and

Francis C. Montague, M.A.

Professor of History, University College, London
Lecturer in Modern History, Oriel College, Oxford

Edited with Notes and Appendices by

James F. Colby

Parker Professor of Law in Dartmouth College

THE LAWBOOK EXCHANGE, LTD.
Clark, New Jersey

ISBN-13: 9781886363502 (hardcover)
ISBN-13: 9781616190675 (paperback)

Lawbook Exchange edition 1998, 2010

The quality of this reprint is equivalent to the quality of the original work.

THE LAWBOOK EXCHANGE, LTD.

33 Terminal Avenue
Clark, New Jersey 07066-1321

*Please see our website for a selection of our other publications
and fine facsimile reprints of classic works of legal history:*
www.lawbookexchange.com

Library of Congress Cataloging-in-Publication Data

Maitland, Frederic William, 1850-1906.
  A sketch of English legal history / by Frederick W. Maitland and
Francis C. Montague : edited with notes and appendices by James F.
Colby.
        p.   cm.
  Originally published : New York : G. P. Putnam's Sons, 1915.
  Includes bibligraphical references and index.
  ISBN 1-886363-50-1 (cloth : alk. paper)
  1. Law—Great Britain—History.   I. Montague, F.C. (Francis
Charles), 1858-1935.   II. Colby, James Fairbanks, 1850-1939.
III. Title.
KD532.M33 1998
349.42'09—dc21
                                                    98-11337
                                                        CIP

Printed in the United States of America on acid-free paper

A Sketch

of

English Legal History

By

Frederic W. Maitland, LL.D., D.C.L.

Late Downing Professor of the Laws of England in the University of Cambridge

and

Francis C. Montague, M.A.

Professor of History, University College, London
Lecturer in Modern History, Oriel College, Oxford

Edited with Notes and Appendices by

James F. Colby

Parker Professor of Law in Dartmouth College

G. P. Putnam's Sons
New York and London
The Knickerbocker Press
1915

The Knickerbocker Press, New York

EDITOR'S NOTE

THE following pages contain a reprint of a series of articles upon the chief epochs in the history of English law which were contributed to *Social England*, edited by H. D. Traill, D.C.L. (G. P. Putnam's Sons, New York, 1899), by the late Prof. Frederic W. Maitland of Cambridge University, and Prof. Francis C. Montague of University College, London. These articles supplied what long had been needed for general readers and for law students—a brief but comprehensive, accurate but untechnical account of the origin and growth of English law. Despite the publication in 1912 of what, by comparison with the voluminous histories of Pollock and Maitland and of Holdsworth, is properly entitled *A Short History of English Law*, by the eminent scholar, Edward Jenks, this series of articles now forms the best available introduction to English legal history. Their original appearance, scattered through the large volumes of *Social England*, has lessened if not barred their use by many persons, and it is hoped that their reprint in this compact form will insure their wider use.

For the benefit of general readers, and particularly

of law students, various explanatory notes have been added. The length of a few such notes, which are extracts from the histories of English law by Pollock and Maitland or by Jenks, has required their insertion in the text, but they always appear within brackets.

A list of recommended readings upon the different topics treated has been appended to each chapter. The references to Pollock and Maitland's *History of English Law* are to the second edition which is cited as "P. and M." *Select Essays in Anglo-American Legal History* is referred to as "Anglo-Am. Legal Hist." The other abbreviations are self-explanatory.

Grateful acknowledgment is hereby made to the several authors specified and to their publishers for their courteous permission to reprint extracts from the volumes below cited:

To Cassell & Co. and the University Press of Cambridge, Eng., for the articles by Maitland and Montague in Traill's *Social England*.

To Little, Brown & Co. of Boston for extracts from *History of English Law* by Pollock and Maitland; *Elements of American Jurisprudence and Elementary Law*, by W. C. Robinson; *A Short History of English Law*, by Edward Jenks.

To Henry Holt & Co. of New York for extracts from *Law and Politics in the Middle Ages*, by Edward Jenks.

Editor's Note

To the Clarendon Press of Oxford, London, and New York for extracts from the monograph by Sir Courtenay Ilbert on *Legislative Methods and Forms.*

The Appendices are designed as supplementary readings upon their several important subjects which are briefly treated in the text, and show the variety of forms which English law has assumed at different epochs during its almost unbroken history from 600 A.D. to the present century.

J. F. C.

HANOVER, N. H.,
August, 1915.

CONTENTS

Contents

Growth of Law. Magna Carta. Statutes of Merton
and Marlbridge. Triumph of Royal Justice. Growth
of the Common Law.

By FREDERIC W. MAITLAND.

Legal Reform under Edward I. Legislation of Edward I.
Growth of a Legal Profession. Attorneys and Barristers.
Serjeants-at-Law. The King's Courts. System of
Writs.

By FREDERIC W. MAITLAND.

The Idea of Law in the Middle Ages. Legislation in
the Fourteenth Century: its Scope. The Omnipotence
of Parliament. Statute and Common Law. The Legal
Profession. The Inns of Court. Growth of the Judicial System. The House of Lords. Beginning of
the Star Chamber: its Work and Use: its Procedure:
its Iniquities. Court of Chancery: its Jurisdiction.
Equity.

By FREDERIC W. MAITLAND.

The Development of Law. Completion of the Common
Law. Independence of the Jury. Bushell's Case.

Contents

A Sketch of English Legal History

A Sketch of English Legal History

CHAPTER I

EARLY ENGLISH LAW, 600–1066 A.D.

Legal History. When we speak of a body of law, we use a metaphor so apt that it is hardly a metaphor. We picture to ourselves a being that lives and grows, that preserves its identity while every atom of which it is composed is subject to a ceaseless process of change, decay, and renewal. At any given moment of time—for example, in the present year—it may, indeed, seem to us that our legislators have, and freely exercise, an almost boundless power of doing what they will with the laws under which we live; and yet we know that, do what they may, their work will become an organic part of an already existing system.

Continuity of English Law. Already, if we look

back at the ages which are the most famous in the history of English legislation—the age of Bentham and the radical reform, the age which appropriated the gains that had been won but not secured under the rule of Cromwell, the age of Henry VIII., the age of Edward I. ("our English Justinian")—it must seem to us that, for all their activity, they changed, and could change, but little in the great body of law which they had inherited from their predecessors. Hardly a rule remains unaltered, and yet the body of law that now lives among us is the same body that Blackstone described in the eighteenth century, Coke in the seventeenth, Littleton in the fifteenth, Bracton in the thirteenth, Glanvill in the twelfth. This continuity, this identity, is very real to us if we know that for the last seven hundred years all the judgments of the courts at Westminster have been recorded, and that for the most part they can still be read.[1] Were the world large enough to contain such a book, we might publish not merely a biography,

[1] "Pleas heard in the King's court (*curia regis*) seem to have been enrolled in the last years of Henry II.'s reign, but the earliest surviving rolls are of the year 1194. (6 Rich. I.)

"From the time of Edward I. onward we have distinct series of records for the King's bench (*coram rege* rolls), common pleas (*de banco rolls*), eyre, gaol-delivery, etc."—Gross, *Sources and Literature of Eng. Hist.*, 352.

The limit of legal memory (Sept. 3, 1189, date of coronation of Richard I.) closely coincides with the written memory of the proceedings of these courts of justice. See Pollock and Maitland, *Hist. of Eng. Law*, (2d ed.) I., 168–9.

but a journal or diary, of English law, telling what it
has done, if not day by day, at least term by term,
ever since the reign of Richard I.; and eventful
though its life may have been, it has had but a single
life.

Beyond these seven centuries there lie six other
centuries that are but partially and fitfully lit, and
in one of them a great catastrophe, the Norman
Conquest, befell England and the law of England.
However, we never quite lose the thread of the story.
Along one path or another we can trace back the
footprints, which have their starting-place in some
settlement of wild Germans who are invading the
soil of Roman provinces, and coming in contact with
the civilization of the old world. Here the trail stops,
the dim twilight becomes darkness; we pass from an
age in which men seldom write their laws, to one in
which they cannot write at all. Beyond lies the
realm of guess-work.

The First English Code. About the year 600,
Æthelbert, King of the Kentings, by the counsel of
his wise men, caused the laws of his people to be set
down in writing. He had just received the Christian
faith at the hands of Roman missionaries, and it was
in imitation of the Romans that he and his folk
desired to have written laws. His reign overlaps the
reign of Justinian, and perhaps he had heard how in
the far east the Roman Emperor had been legislating

on a magnificent scale. English law begins to speak just when Roman law has spoken what will, in a certain sense, be its final words.[1] On the Continent of Europe the same thing had been happening. No sooner did the barbarian tribe feel the influence of Rome than it wished for a written code of laws. Æthelbert and his Jutes in Kent are doing what the Salian Franks did a century ago when they wrote down their famous Lex Salica[2]; but while on the Continent the laws of the conquering Germans are written in the Latin language of the conquered, in England the barbarians from the first write down their law in the language that they speak, the language which is to become English.

Christian Influences. Æthelbert's laws[3] have come down to us, though only in a copy made after the Norman Conquest. They may seem to us primi-

---

[1] The *Corpus Juris Civilis* which embodied the Roman law in the form which it assumed a thousand years after the decemviral legislation of the Twelve Tables, 450 B.C., and through which mainly it has influenced modern times, was compiled under Justinian and published in 529–34 A.D.

[2] A Frankish code named from the Salians, a people of Germany who settled in Gaul. If not the oldest, the Lex Salica is still one of the earliest extant statements of Germanic custom, dating probably from the reign of Chlodwig, 486–511. Though written in Latin it is very free from the Roman taint. Like other Germanic folk-laws it consists largely of a tariff of offences and atonements. We have no more instructive document and, by virtue of the Norman Conquest, the Lex is one of the ancestors of English law.—P. and M., *Hist. of Eng. Law*, I., 6–7.

[3] For laws of Æthelbert, see Appendix I.

tive enough. The emperor at Byzantium, could he
have seen them, would assuredly have denied that
they had any points in common with the Roman
law-books, save that they were laws, and were in
writing. Nevertheless, we cannot call them primi-
tive in any absolute sense of that term. They are
Christian.

Let us look at the first sentence, the first recorded
utterance of English law: "God's fee[1] [property]
and the church's, twelve-fold; bishop's fee, eleven-
fold; priest's fee, nine-fold; deacon's fee, six-fold;
clerk's fee, three-fold." Churches, bishops, priests,
deacons, clerks—these are no archaic German institutions; they are Latin, they have Latin names which
must be taken up bodily into the Teutonic speech
of the new converts. Unfortunately (so we may now
think) Germanic law has no written memorials of the
days of its heathenry. Every trace, but the very
faintest, of the old religion has been carefully ex-
purgated from all that is written, for all that is
written passes under ecclesiastical hands. Thus we
may guess that a new force is already beginning to
transfigure the whole sum and substance of barbaric
law, before that law speaks the first words that we
can hear. It is a wild plant that has already been

---

[1] The Anglo-Saxon word, *feoh, fee* (property), sometimes is
rendered cattle. For explanation of this doom so translated, see
Jenks, *Law and Politics in the Middle Ages*, 191-4.

torn from its native soil and set to grow in a garden. The change of faith, and the substitution of one order of religious rites for another, would in any case mean much, for we have reason to believe that the old law had in it a strong sacral element; but as it is, they mean the influence of the old civilized world upon the new barbarian world.

Æthelbert's laws consist of ninety brief sentences. Two will serve as samples: "If one man strike another with the fist on the nose—three shillings." "If the eye be struck out let boot [*i. e.*, amends] be made with fifty shillings." To call this brief tariff a code may seem strange, but there are not wanting signs that the wise-men of Kent are committing to writing as much of their traditional law as they can remember in the form of abstract propositions. No doubt much more law—in particular, a law of procedure[1]— is known to them implicitly. If a concrete case were to occur, they would be ready with a doom [judgment]; but when asked for general rules, these ninety are all that they can call to mind. Thus we may say that our legal history starts with an act of codification. This code became the basis of Kentish law. Subsequent kings in the course of the seventh century, Hlothar, Eadric, Wihtræd, with the counsel of

[1] The method of conducting legislation and judicial proceedings. Procedure now commonly includes in its meaning whatever is embraced by the three technical terms, pleading, evidence, and practice.—Bouvier's *Law Dict.*

the wise, add some fifty new dooms to the written
law of the men of Kent. Then the scene changes to
Wessex.

The Laws of Ine. In the middle of the seventh
century the West Saxons received Christianity;
before its end they had written laws, the laws of
Ine[1] (688–726). By the advice of his bishops and
of the oldest and wisest men, Ine published a set
of laws which tell us a good deal more than we can
learn from the Kentish series.

Alfred's Legislation. The next legislator whose
work has come down to us is the great Alfred[2] (871–
901). His laws are divided from those of his ancestor
Ine by a period of two centuries or thereabouts.
This is the one great gap in our continuous legal
history. In the history of religion and learning and
letters these centuries are far from being the darkest.
They cover the time when Northumbria was for a
while a centre of light—not for England only, but
for the world at large. It may be that we have lost
some things. It is fairly certain that Offa (757–96)
of Mercia, in the days of Mercia's greatness, issued
written laws. When Alfred is King, when all England

[1] For laws of Ine (about 690), see Thorpe, *Ancient Laws and
Institutes of England*, I., 103–51, London, 1840.

[2] For laws of Alfred, see Thorpe, *Ancient Laws and Institutes of
England*, I., 45–101.

For brief bibliography on Alfred's laws and discussion of manuscripts, sources, and probable date, see *Legal Code of Alfred the Great*,
edited by M. H. Turk, Boston, 1893.

is becoming united under the vigorous princes of the West Saxon house, the three legislators whose names are still remembered are Æthelbert of Kent, Ine of Wessex, and Offa of Mercia. From the manner in which Alfred speaks of them and of their laws we may gather that, heavy though our losses may have been, we have lost no document that testified to any revolutionary change in the law. Though near three hundred years have gone by since Æthelbert's death, his dooms are still in force among the Kentish people. Alfred tells us that he dared to add but little of his own to the work of his three great forerunners; and though we can see that during the last two centuries some new legal ideas have emerged, still the core of the law is what it was.[1] What can be put in writing is for the more part a tariff of the sums that must be paid when deeds of violence are done.

The Alfred of sober truth is not the Alfred of legal

---

[1] The preface to these laws, evidently dictated by Alfred himself, reads as follows:

"I, then, Alfred, King, gathered these together, and commanded many of those to be written which our forefathers held, those which to me seemed good; and many of those which seemed to me not good I rejected them, by the counsel of my 'witan,' and in other wise commanded them to be holden; for I durst not venture to set down in writing much of my own, for it was unknown to me what of it would please those who should come after us. But those things which I met with, either of the days of Ine my kinsman, or of Offa King of the Mercians, or of Æthelbryght, who first among the English race received baptism, those which seemed to me the rightest, those I have here gathered together, and rejected the others."— Thorpe, *Ancient Laws and Institutes of England*, I., 59.

legend—for the history of law has its legends—the inventive architect of a British Constitution; but his laws are the first member of a grand series—the capitularies,[1] we might call them, of the English kings of the West Saxon house. Edward the Elder, Æthelstan, Edmund, and Edgar, with the counsel of their wise-men, legislate in a bold, masterful fashion. For the better maintenance of the peace, they sharpen the old rules and they make new rules. Written law accumulates somewhat rapidly; it is expected by this time that the doomsmen will be able to find in the "doom-book," the book of written law, judgments apt for most of the cases which come before them. This series extends from the beginning to the end of the tenth century. The laws of Æthelred continue it into the eleventh century. His laws were many, for he had to say the same thing over and over again; we can see on their face that they were ineffectual. He begs and prays men to keep the peace and desist from crime; he must beg and pray, for he cannot command and punish. The Danes were ravaging and conquering; the State tottered; the house of Cerdic fell.

Canute. It was left for the mighty Canute (1017–

---

[1] "A collection of ordinances (in modern law called *capitula*), especially those made in their own authority by the Frankish kings."—*Cent. Dict.*

In French law, "a collection of laws and ordinances orderly arranged by divisions."—Bouvier's *Law Dict.*

35) to bring to a noble close the first great period in
the history of English law, the period during which
laws were written in the English language, the period
which it is convenient to call Anglo-Saxon. Canute's
code we must, if we have regard to the age in which it
was issued, call a long and a comprehensive code.[1]
It repeats, with improvements, things that have
been said before; the great Dane was able to enforce
as laws rules which in the mouth of his predecessor
had been little better than pious wishes; but it also
contained many things that had not been said before.
The whole economic and political structure of society
was undergoing a great change. If by any two words
we could indicate the nature of this elaborate process,
we might say that tribalism was giving place to
feudalism. Had Canute's successors been his equals
in vigour and wisdom, perhaps the change might
have been consummated peacefully, and by means of
written laws which we might now be reading. As
it was, there came to the throne the holy but imbecile
Edward.

[**Anglo-Saxon Justice.** The impotence of the
growing English State in the administration of justice during the Anglo-Saxon period is thus described
by Sir Frederick Pollock:

---

[1] For laws of Canute, see Thorpe, *Ancient Laws and Institutes of
Eng.*, I., 359–430. For brief description of these laws, see Freeman,
Hist. Norman Conquest of Eng. (Am. ed.), 1873, I., 291–2.

"Rigid and cumbrous as Anglo-Saxon justice was in the things it did provide for, it was, to modern eyes, strangely defective in its lack of executive power. Among the most important functions of courts as we know them is compelling the attendance of parties and enforcing the fulfilment both of final judgments and of interlocutory orders dealing with the conduct of proceedings and the like. Such things are done as of course under the ordinary authority of the court, and with means constantly at its disposal; open resistance to judicial orders is so plainly useless it is seldom attempted, and obstinate preference of penalties to submission, a thing which now and then happens, is counted a mark of eccentricity bordering on unsoundness of mind. Exceptional difficulties, when they occur, indicate an abnormal state of the commonwealth or some of its members. But this reign of law did not come by nature; it has been slowly and laboriously won. Jurisdiction began, it seems, with being merely voluntary, derived not from the authority of the State but from the consent of the parties. People might come to the court for a decision if they agreed to do so. They were bound in honour to accept the result; they might forfeit pledges deposited with the court; but the court could not compel their obedience any more than a tribunal of arbitration appointed at this day under a treaty between sovereign

States can compel the rulers of those States to fulfil its award. Anglo-Saxon courts had got beyond this most early stage, but not very far beyond it.

"The only way to bring an unwilling adversary before the court was to take something of his as security till he would attend to the demand; and practically the only things that could be taken without personal violence were cattle. Distress in this form was practised and also regulated from a very early time. It was forbidden to distrain until right had been formally demanded—in Cnut's time to the extent of three summonings—and refused. Thus leave of the court was required, but the party had to act for himself as best he could. If distress failed to make the defendant appear, the only resource left was to deny the law's protection to the stiff-necked man who would not come to be judged by law. He might be outlawed, and this must have been enough to coerce most men who had anything to lose and were not strong enough to live in rebellion; but still no right could be done to the complainant without his submission. The device of a judgment by default, which is familiar enough to us, was unknown, and probably would not have been understood.

"Final judgment, when obtained, could in like manner not be directly enforced. The successful party had to see to gathering the 'fruits of judgment,' as we say, for himself. In case of continued refusal to do right according to the sentence of the court, he might take the law into his own hands, in fact wage war on his obstinate opponent. The earl-dorman's aid, and ultimately the king's, could be invoked in such extreme cases as that of a wealthy man, or one backed by a powerful family, setting the law at open defiance. But this was an extraor-dinary measure, analogous to nothing in the regular modern process of law."]—Pollock's *Expansion of the Common Law*, 145–6.

The Laws of the Confessor. In after-days he won not only the halo of the saint, to which he may have been entitled, but the fame, to which he cer-tainly was not entitled, of having been a great legislator. In the minster that he reared, king after king made oath to observe the laws of the Confessor. So far as we know, he never made a law. Had he made laws, had he even made good use of those that were already made, there might have been no Nor-man Conquest of England. But then had there been no Norman Conquest of England, Edward would never have gained his fictitious glories. As it was, men looked back to him as the last of the English kings of the English—for of Harold, who had become the perjured usurper, there could be no talk—and galled by the yoke of their French masters, they sighed for Saint Edward's law, meaning thereby the law that had prevailed in a yet unvanquished England.

Contrast of Ancient and Modern Statutes. Now these enacted and written laws of our forefathers, representing as they do some four centuries and a half, representing as long a period as that which divides us from the Wars of the Roses, will seem a small thing to the first glance of a modern eye. They might all be handsomely printed on a hundred pages such as that which is now before the reader. A session of Parliament which produced no larger mass of matter we should nowadays regard as a sterile session. In the Georgian age many more words than are contained in the whole code of Canute would have been devoted to the modest purpose of paving and lighting the borough of Little Peddlington. It is but fair to our ancient kings and their wisemen to say that when they spoke, they spoke briefly and pointedly. They had no fear that ingenious lawyers would turn their words inside out. "God's fee and the Church's, twelve-fold"—they feel that they need say no more than this about one very important matter. Also we have to remember that life was simple; men could do, men could wish to do, but few things. Our increasing mastery over the physical world is always amplifying the province of law, for it is always complicating the relationships which exist between human beings. Many a modern Act of Parliament is the product of the steam-engine, and there is no great need for a law of copyright

until long after the printing-press has begun its
work. For all this, however, it is true that these old
written and enacted dooms contain but a part of the
law which was enforced in England.

If we say that law serves three great purposes,
that it punishes crime, redresses wrong, and decides
disputes—and perhaps we need not go into the
matter more deeply than this—then we may go on to
say that in ancient days the first two of these three
purposes are indistinguishably blended, while with
the third the legislator seldom troubles himself.
If he can maintain the peace, suppress violence and
theft, keep vengeance within moderate bounds, he is
well satisfied; he will not be at pains to enact a law
of contract[1] or of inheritance, a law of husband and

[1] "There was not any law of contract at all, as we now understand
it. The two principal kinds of transaction requiring the exchange or
acceptance of promises to be performed in the future were marriage
and the payment of wergild. Apart from the general sanctions of
the Church, and the king's special authority where his peace had
been declared, the only ways of adding any definite security to a
promise were oath and giving of pledges. One or both of these were
doubtless regularly used on solemn occasions like the settlement of a
blood-feud; and we may guess that the oath, which at all events
carried a spiritual sanction, was freely resorted to for various purposes. But business had hardly got beyond delivery against ready
money between parties both present, and there was not much room
for such confidence as that on which, for example, the existence of
modern banking rests. How far the popular law took any notice of
petty trading disputes, such as there were, we are not informed; it
seems likely that for the most part they were left to be settled by
special customs of traders, and possibly by special local tribunals in
towns and markets. Merchants trafficking beyond seas, in any case,
must have relied on the customs of their trade and order rather than

wife, a law of landlord and tenant. All this can
safely be left to unwritten tradition. He has no
care to satisfy the curiosity of a remote posterity
which will come prying into these affairs and wish to
write books about them. Thus, to take one example,
the courts must have been ready to decide disputes
about the property of dead men; there must have
been a general law, or various tribal or local laws, of
inheritance.[1]   But the lawgivers tell us nothing
about this. If we would recover the old rules, we
must make the best that we may of stray hints and
chance stories, and of those archaisms which we find
embedded in the law of later days.

Folk-right. The laws of the folk, the "folk-right"
—"law" is one of those words which the Danes
bring with them—is known to the men of the folk,
but more especially to the old and wise. The free-
men, or the free landowners, of the hundred are in
duty bound to frequent the "moot," or court of the

---

the cumbrous formal justice of the time."—Pollock, "English Law
before the Norman Conquest," in *Law Quar. Review*, July, 1898, 303.
Reprinted in his *Expansion of the Common Law*, 155–6.

[1] Reference to such a law which apparently had become general
before Canute's day is found in his laws:

"If any one leaves this world without a cwiðe," (variously rendered a saying, a dictum, last-words, intestate), "be this due to his
negligence or to sudden death, then let the lord take naught from his
property save his right heriot (military apparel); and let the property
be distributed according to his (the lord's) direction and according
to law among the wife and children and nearest kinsfolk, to each the
proper share."—P. and M., *Hist. of Eng. Law*, II., 322.

hundred,[1] to declare the law and to make the dooms. The presiding ealdorman or sheriff turns to them when a statement of the law is wanted. As yet there is no class of professional lawyers, but the work of attending the courts is discharged chiefly by men of substance, men of thegnly rank[2]; the small folk are glad to stay at home.

Characteristics of Early Law. Also some men acquire a great reputation for legal learning, and there was much to be learnt, though no one thought

[1] "The ordinary Anglo-Saxon courts of public justice were the county court and the hundred court, of which the county court was appointed to be held twice a year, the hundred every four weeks."
—P. and M., *Hist. of Eng. Law*, I., 42.

For full description of these courts, see *idem*, I., 532–60; also Henry Adams on Anglo-Saxon Courts of Law in *Essays on Anglo-Saxon Law*.

[2] "The official term of rank which we find in use in and after Alfred's time is 'thane'. Originally a thane is a household officer of some great man, eminently and especially of the king. From the tenth century to the Conquest thaneship is not an office unless described by some specific addition showing what the office was. It is a social condition above that of the churl, carrying with it both privileges and customary duties. The king's thanes, those who are in fact attached to the king's person and service, are especially distinguished. We may perhaps roughly compare the thanes of the later Anglo-Saxon monarchy to the country gentlemen of modern times who are in the commission of the peace and serve in the grand jury. But we must remember that the thane had a definite legal rank. His wergild for example, the fixed sum with which his death must be atoned for to his kindred, or which he might in some cases have to pay for his own misdoing, was six times as great as a common man's; and his oath weighed as much more in the curious contest of asseverations, quite different from anything we now understand by evidence, by which early Germanic lawsuits were decided."—P. and M., *Hist. of Eng. Law*, I., 33.

of setting it in writing. We should assuredly make a great mistake were we to picture to ourselves these old moots as courts of equity, where "the natural man" administered an informal "law of Nature." For one thing, as will be said elsewhere, the law of the natural man is supernatural law, a law which deals in miracles and portents. But then, again, it is exceedingly formal. It is a law of procedure. The right words must be said without slip or trip, the due ceremonial acts must be punctiliously performed, or the whole transaction will go for naught. This is the main theme of the wise-man's jurisprudence. One suspects that sometimes the man, who in the estimate of his neighbours has become very wise indeed, has it in his power to amplify tradition by devices of his own. We hear from Iceland a wonderful tale of a man so uniquely wise that though he had made himself liable to an action of a particular kind, no one could bring that action against him, for he and only he knew the appropriate words of summons: to trick him into a disclosure of this precious formula is a feat worthy of a hero. But formalism has its admirable as well as its ludicrous side. So long as law is unwritten, it must be dramatized and acted. Justice must assume a picturesque garb, or she will not be seen. And even of chicane we may say a good word, for it is the homage which lawlessness pays to law.

Fine and Composition. We have called the written laws "tariffs." They prescribe in great detail the various sums of money which must be paid by wrong-doers. There are payments to be made to the injured person or to the kinsfolk of the slain man; there are also payments to be made to the king, or to some other representative of the tribe or nation. The growth of this system of pecuniary mulcts gradually restricts the sphere of self-help and vengeance. The tie of blood-relationship has been the straitest of all bonds of union. If a man of one family was slain by the man of another, there would be a blood-feud, a private war. The State steps in and compels the injured family to accept the dead man's wergild—the dead man's price or worth, if it be duly tendered. King Edmund (945–6) goes so far as to insist that the vengeance of the dead man's kinsfolk is not to comprise the guiltless members of the slayer's clan. The law's last weapon against lawlessness is outlawry.[1] The contumacious offender is put outside the peace; he becomes the foe of all law-abiding men. It is their duty to waste his land and burn his house, to pursue him and knock him on the head as though he were a beast of prey, for "he bears the wolf's head." As the State grows stronger,

[1] P. and M., *Hist. of Eng. Law*, I., 49, 476–8; Blackstone, *Com.*, III., 283; Jenks, *Law and Politics in Mid. Ages* (see "Ban" in Index).

less clumsy modes of punishment become possible;
the criminal can be brought to trial, and definitely
sentenced to death or mutilation.   We can watch a
system of true punishments—corporeal and capital
punishments—growing at the expense of the old
system of pecuniary mulcts, blood-feud, and outlawry; but on the eve of the Norman Conquest mere
homicide can still be atoned for by the payment of
the dead man's price or wergild,[1] and if that be not
paid, it is rather for the injured family than for the
State to slay the slayer.   Men of different ranks had
different prices: the thegn was worth six ceorls, and
it seems very plain that if a ceorl killed a thegn, he
had to die for it, or was sold into slavery, for a
thegnly wergild was quite beyond the reach of his
modest means.   In the twelfth century the old

---

[1] "The principle that every injury either to person or property
might be compensated by a money payment was common to all the
northern nations.   It was introduced into Gaul by the conquering
Franks, and into Britain by the English invaders.   Every man's
life had a fixed money value, called the *wergild*.   In the case of a
freeman, this compensation for murder was payable to his kindred;
and that of a slave to his master.   The amount of the wergild varied,
according to a graduated scale, with the rank of the person slain.
For a ceorl it was fixed at 200 shillings; for a lesser thegn, 600 shillings;
for a king's thegn, 1200 shillings.   The wer of an earldorman was
double that of a king's thegn; that of an atheling three times, that
of a king usually six times as much."—Taswell-Langmead, *Eng.
Consti. Hist.*, 5th ed., 34.   See P. and M., *Hist. of Eng. Law*, I., 48,
74; II., 241–3, 450, 459–60.

For full treatment of this subject, see Seebohm's *Tribal Custom in
Anglo-Saxon Law*.

system perished of over-elaboration. The bill that a manslayer ran up became in the days of feudalism too complex to be summed, too heavy to be paid; for the dead man's lord, the lord of the place where the blood was shed, and it may be many other lords, would claim fines and forfeitures. He had to pay with his eyes or with his life a debt that he could not otherwise discharge.

The Influence of Rome. As yet our Germanic law had not been exposed to the assaults of Roman jurisprudence, but still it had been slowly assuming and assimilating the civilization of the old world. This distinction we must draw. On the one hand, there has been no borrowing from the Roman legal texts. We have no proof whatever that during the five centuries which preceded the Norman Conquest any one copy of a Roman law-book existed in England. We hear faint and vague tidings of law being taught in some of the schools, but may safely believe that very little is meant thereby. The written dooms of our kings have been searched over and over again by men skilled in detecting the least shred of Roman law under the most barbaric disguise, and they have found nothing worthy of mention. That these dooms are the purest specimens of pure Germanic law has been the verdict of one scholar after another. Even the English Church, though its independence may often have been exaggerated, became very

English. On the other hand, as already said, to become Christian was in a certain sense to become Roman. Whether, had an impassable wall been raised round England in the last quarter of the sixth century, England would not be a barbarous country at this day—that is a question which cannot be answered. As a matter of fact, we had not to work out our own civilization; we could adopt results already attained in the ancient world. For example, we did not invent the art of writing, we adopted it; we did not invent our alphabet, we took the Roman. And so again—to come nearer to our law—we borrowed or inherited from the old world the written legal document, the written conveyance, the will. The written conveyance was introduced along with Christianity; to all seeming Æthelbert himself began the practice of "booking"[1] lands to the churches. We have a few genuine "land-books" from the seventh and eighth, many from the later centuries. For the more part they are written in Latin, and they were fashioned after Italian models; but at the same time we can see that those models have been barbarized and misunderstood; the English scribes

[1] "Our Anglo-Saxon charters or *books* are usually grants of considerable portions of land made by kings to bishoprics and religious houses, or to lay nobles. Land so granted was called book-land, and the grant confined a larger dominion than was known to the popular customary law. During the ninth century and the early part of the tenth the grant usually purports to be with the consent of the witan." —P. and M., *Hist of Eng. Law*, I., 60.

pervert the neat devices of Roman lawyers. Any phrase which draws a contrast between a nation's law and its civilisation is of course open to objection. But let us suppose that at the present day a party of English missionaries is setting forth to convert a savage tribe: perhaps no one of them would know enough of English law to carry him through the easiest examination, and yet they would take with them many ideas that are in a certain sort the ideas of English law. Without being able to define murder, they would know that in this country murderers are condemned to death; they would think that a written expression of a man's last will should be respected, though they might well doubt whether a will is revoked by the testator's marriage. So it was in the seventh century. From the days of Æthelbert onwards English law was under the influence of so much of Roman law as had worked itself into the tradition of the Catholic Church.

READINGS

On Outlines of Legal History of Europe during the Middle Ages:
Maitland, "A Prologue to a History of English Law," *Law Quar. Rev.*, XIV., 1898, reprinted in P. and M., *Hist. of Eng. Law*, I., ch. i. (The Dark Age in Legal History); also in *Anglo-Am. Legal Hist.*, I., ch. i.; Sohm, R., *Institutes of Roman Law*, 1-97, trans. from 4th Ger. ed.; Hunter, W. A., *Roman Law*, 90-93, 98-116; Morey, *Outlines of Roman Law*, 167-92; Jenks, Edw., *Law and Politics in Mid. Ages.*

On the Germanic Origin of English Legal Institutions:
Stubbs, *Eng. Consti. Hist.*, I., chaps. ii., iii., iv.; Taswell-Langmead, *Eng. Consti. Hist.*, ch. i., 1-7.

On the Anglo-Saxon Law:
Stubbs, *Consti. Hist. of Eng.*, I., chaps. v., vi.; *Select Charters*, 60-1; P. and M., *Hist of Eng. Law*, I., ch. ii.; Holdsworth, *Hist. of Eng. Law*, II., bk. i.; Pollock, F., "Eng. Law before the Norman Conquest," *Law Quar. Rev.*, XIV., 1898, reprinted in his *Expansion of the Common Law*, 139-58, also in *Anglo-Am. Legal Hist.*, I., ch. iii.; Taswell-Langmead, *Eng. Consti. Hist.*, ch. i.; Stephen, *Hist. of Crim. Law of Eng.*, I., ch. iii. For summary account of Anglo-Saxon Laws, see Gross, *Sources and Literature of Eng. Hist.*, 195-8. For text of Anglo-Saxon Laws, see Thorpe, *Ancient Laws and Institutes of Eng.*, London, 1840; Schmid, Reinhold, *Die Gesetze der Angelsachsen*, 2d ed., Leipsic, 1858; Liebermann, Felix, *Die Gesetze der Angelsachsen im Auftrage der Savigny-Stiftung*, Halle, 1903-12. 3 vols.

On Early English Family Law:
P. and M., *Hist. of Eng. Law*, II., ch. vii.; Holdsworth, *Hist. of Eng. Law*, II., bk. i., pt. ii., 75-78.

24

On Early English Law of Inheritance:
P. and M., *Hist. of Eng. Law*, II., 250–62, 318–25; Holdsworth, *Hist. of Eng. Law*, II., bk. i., pt. ii., 78–87; Jenks, *Law and Politics in Mid. Ages*, 225–34.

On Origin and Growth of English Law of Contract:
Holmes, *Com. Law*, ch. vii.; P. and M., *Hist. of Eng. Law*, II., ch. v.; Jenks, *Law and Politics in Mid. Ages*, ch. vii.; Holdsworth, *Hist. of Eng. Law*, II., bk. i., pt. ii., 72–75.

On Characteristics of Early Law:
Maine, Henry, *Ancient Law*, chaps., i.–iii., and *Early Hist. of Insti.;* Lea, Henry C., *Superstition and Force;* Holmes, *Common Law*, Lecture I.; Bigelow, Melville M., *Hist. of Procedure in Eng.*

CHAPTER II

ENGLISH LAW UNDER NORMAN RULE AND THE
LEGAL REFORMS OF HENRY II., 1066–1216

English Law under Norman Rule. The Normans
when they invaded England were in one important
particular a less civilized race than were those
English whom they came to subjugate. We may
say with some certainty that they had no written
laws. A century and a half ago a king of the Franks
had been compelled to cede a large province to a
horde of Scandinavian pirates. The pirates had
settled down as lords of a conquered people; they
had gradually adopted the religion, the language,
and the civilization (such as it was) of the vanquished;
they had become Frenchmen. They may have paid
some reverence to the written laws of the Frankish
race, to the very ancient Lex Salica and the capitularies of Merovingian and Carlovingian kings. But
these were fast becoming obsolete, and neither the
dukes of the Normans, nor their nominal overlords,
the kings of the Franks or French, could issue written
dooms such as those which Canute was publishing

in England. Some excellent traditions of a far-off
past, of the rule of Charles the Great (800–14), the
invaders could bring with them to England; and
these, transplanted into the soil of a subject kingdom,
could burst into new life and bear new fruit—the
great record that we call "Domesday Book" is a
splendid firstfruit—but written laws they had none.

To all seeming, the Conqueror meant that his
English subjects should keep their own old laws.
Merely Duke of the Normans, he was going to be
King in England, and he was not dissatisfied with
those royal rights which, according to his version of
the story, had descended to him from King Edward.
About a few points he legislated. For example, the
lives of his followers were to be protected by the
famous murder-fine. If a Frenchman was found
slain, and the slayer was not produced, a heavy sum
was to be exacted from the district in which the crime
was done. The establishment of a presumption that
every murdered man is a Frenchman until the contrary is proved—a presumption highly advantageous
to the King's exchequer—gave rise in later days to
the curious process known as the "presentment of
Englishry."[1] The hundred had to pay the fine unless

---

[1] "Presentments of Englishry, as they were technically termed,
are recorded in the reign of Richard I., but not later. Even so early as
the reign of Henry II., we are told that the two races (with the exceptions of the villeins) had become so blended through inter-
marriages, that the distinction between Norman and Englishman

the kinsfolk of the dead man would testify to his English birth. But this by the way. William had also to regulate the scope of that trial by battle which the Normans brought with them, and in so doing he tried to deal equitably with both Normans and English. Also it was necessary that he who had come hither as in some sort the champion of Roman orthodoxy should mark off the sphere of spiritual from that of temporal law by stricter lines than had yet been drawn in England. Much, again—though by no general law—he altered in the old military system, which had lately shown itself to be miserably ineffectual. Dealing out the forfeited lands among his barons, he could stipulate for a force of armoured and mounted knights. Some other changes he would make; but in the main he was content that the English should live under their old law, the law that now bore the blessed Edward's name.

Law under Henry I. And so again when on the death of Rufus—from Rufus himself we get and we expect no laws—Henry seized the crown, and was compelled to purchase adherents by granting a charter full of all manner of promises, made to all

---

had almost entirely disappeared."—Taswell-Langmead, *Eng. Consti. Hist.*, 57.

Presentment of Englishry was abolished by statute of 14 Ed. III., 1340.

For definition of Englishry and its abolition, see Stephen, *Hist. of Crim. Law of Eng.*, III., 31, 40.

manner of people—the promise by which he hoped
to win the hearts of Englishmen was that he would
restore to them Edward's law with those amendments
that the Conqueror had made in it. Henry himself,
great as a governor, was no great legislator. A
powerful central tribunal, which is also an exacting
financial bureau, an "exchequer," began to take
definite shape under the management of his expert
ministers; but very few new laws were published.
The most characteristic legal exploits of the Norman
period are the attempts made by various private
persons to reconstruct "the law of St. Edward."
They translate some of the old English dooms into
Latin as best they can—a difficult task, for the
English language is rapidly taking a new shape.
They modify the old dooms to suit a new age. They
borrow from foreign sources—from the canon law
of the Catholic Church, from Frankish capitularies,
now and again from the Roman law-books. But in
Henry I.'s reign they still regard the old English
dooms, the law of King Edward, as the core of the
law that prevails in England. They leave us wonder-
ing how much practical truth there is in what they
say; whether the ancient criminal tariffs that they
transcribe are really observed; whether the Frenchmen who preside in court pay much attention to the
words of Canute, even when those words have been
turned into Latin or into French. Still, their efforts

assure us that there has been rather a dislocation than a complete break in the legal history of England; also that the Frenchmen have not introduced much new law of a sufficiently definite kind to be set down in writing.

As yet the great bulk of all the justice that was done, was done by local courts, by those shire-moots and hundred-moots which the Conqueror and Henry I. had maintained as part of the ancient order, and by the newer seignorial courts[1] which were springing up in every village. The king's own court was but a court for the protection of royal rights, a court for the causes of the king's barons, and an ultimate tribunal at which a persistent litigant might perhaps arrive when justice had failed him everywhere else. Had it continued to be no more than this, the Old English law, slowly adapting itself to changed circumstances, might have cast off its archaisms and become the law for after-times, law to be written and spoken in English words. Far more probably "St. Edward's law" would have split into a myriad local customs, and then at some future time Englishmen must have found relief from intolerable con-

---

[1] A domestic court (sometimes known as a Court Baron), incident to every manor, to be held by the steward within the manor, for redressing misdemeanors and nuisances therein, and for settling disputes among the tenants relating to property. It is not a court of record.—Bouvier's *Law Dictionary*; Blackstone, *Com.*, II., 90; Medley, *Eng. Consti. Hist.*, 310–16; Vinogradoff, *Growth of the Manor.*

fusion in the eternal law of Rome. Neither of these two things happened, because under Henry II. (1154–89) the king's own court flung open its doors to all manner of people, ceased to be for judicial purposes an occasional assembly of warlike barons, became a bench of professional justices, appeared periodically in all the counties of England under the guise of the Justices in Eyre.[1]

Then begins the process which makes the custom of the king's court the common law of England. Ever since the Conquest the king's court had been in a very true sense a French court. It had been a French-speaking court, a court whose members had been of French race, and had but slowly been learning to think of themselves as Englishmen. Its hands had been very free. It could not, if it would, have administered the old English written laws in their native purity: for one thing they were unintelligible; for another thing in the twelfth century they had become barbarous—they dealt with crime in a hopelessly old-fashioned way. On the other part, there was, happily, no written Norman code, and the king did not mean to be in England the mere duke he had

[1] "The system of Itinerant Justices or Justices in Eyre was not invented by Henry II., but its establishment as an organized and permanent institution is due to him. As early as the reign of Henry I. some of the justices of the Curia Regis were occasionally appointed by the king to go from county to county to collect the revenue and hold pleas, civil and criminal."—Taswell-Langmead, *Eng. Consti. Hist.*, 131.

been in Normandy. And so the hands of his court were very free; it could be a law unto itself. Many old English institutions it preserved, in particular those institutions of public law which were advantageous to the king—the king, for instance, could insist that the sheriffs were sheriffs, and not hereditary *vicomtes*—but the private law, law of land tenure, law of possession, of contract, of procedure, which the court develops in the course of the twelfth century, is exceedingly like a *coutume*[1] from Northern France. Hundreds of years will elapse before any one tries to write about it in English; and when at length this is done, the English will be an English in which every important noun, every accurate term, is of French origin.

Legal Language. We may say a little more about the language of our law, for it is a not uninteresting topic. From the Conquest onwards until the year 1731 the solemnest language of our law was neither French nor English, but Latin. Even in the

---

[1] *Coutume* signifies ancient and general usage, having the force of law.

"The very name Common Law seems to imply some kind of reference to general usage and acceptance as being the ultimate claim of the law upon the individual citizen's allegiance. In short, the Common Law is a customary law if, in the course of about six centuries, the undoubting belief and uniform language of everybody who had occasion to consider the matter were able to make it so. To this day *coutume* is the nearest equivalent that learned Frenchmen can find for its English name."—Pollock, *First Book on Juris.*, 240.

Anglo-Saxon time, though English was the language in which laws were published, and causes were pleaded, Latin was the language in which the kings, with Italian models before them, made grants of land to the churches and the thegns. In 1066 the learned men of both races could write and speak to each other in Latin. We shall be pretty safe in saying that any one who could read and write at all could read and write Latin. As to French, it was as yet little better than a vulgar dialect of Latin, a language in which men might speak, but not a language in which they would write anything, except perhaps a few songs. The two tongues which the Conqueror used for laws, charters, and writs, were Latin and English. But Latin soon gets the upper hand, and becomes for a while the one written language of the law. In the king's Chancery they write nothing but Latin, and it is in Latin that the judgments of the king's courts are recorded. This, as already said, is so until the year 1731; to substitute English for Latin as the language in which the king's writs and patents and charters shall be expressed, and the doings of the law-courts shall be preserved, requires a statute of George II.'s day.

Meanwhile there had been many and great changes. Late in the twelfth or early in the thirteenth century French was beginning to make itself a language in which not only songs and stories but legal documents

3

could be written. About the middle of the thirteenth
century ordinances and statutes that are written in
French begin to appear. Just for one moment
English puts in a claim to equality. Henry III.
"þurȝ Godes fultume king on Engleneloande"
issued one proclamation in English. But this claim
was either belated or premature. Under Edward I.
French, though it cannot expel Latin from the
records of litigation, becomes the language in which
laws are published and law-books are written. It
continues to be the language of the statute-book
until the end of the Middle Ages. Under Henry
VII. English at length becomes the speech in which
English lawgivers address their subjects, though
some two hundred and fifty years must yet pass
away before it will win that field in which Latin is
securely entrenched.

As the oral speech of litigants and their advisers,
French has won a splendid victory. In the king's
own court it must prevail from the Conquest onwards, but in the local courts a great deal of English
must long have been spoken. Then, however, under
Henry II. began that centralizing movement which
we have already noticed. The jurisprudence of a
French-speaking court became the common law,
the measure of all rights and duties, and it was
carried throughout the land by the journeying
justices.

In the thirteenth century men, when they plead or when they talk about law, speak French; the professional lawyer writes in French and thinks in French. Some power of speaking a decent French seems to have been common among all classes of men, save the very poorest; men spoke it who had few, if any, drops of foreign blood in their veins. Then in 1362, when the prolonged wars between England and France had begun, a patriotic statute endeavoured to make English instead of French the spoken tongue of the law-courts. But this came too late; we have good reason for thinking that it was but tardily obeyed, and, at any rate, lawyers went on writing about law in French. Gradually in the sixteenth century their French went to the bad, and they began to write in English; for a long time past they had been thinking and speaking in English. But it was an English in which almost all the technical terms were of French origin. And so it is at the present day. How shall one write a single sentence about law without using some such word as "debt," "contract," "heir," "trespass," "pay," "money," "court," "judge," "jury"? But all these words have come to us from the French. In all the world-wide lands where English law prevails, homage is done daily to William of Normandy and Henry of Anjou.

Henry II.'s Legal Reforms. What Henry did in the middle of the twelfth century was of the utmost importance, though we might find ourselves in the midst of obsolete technicalities were we to endeavour to describe it at length. Speaking briefly, we may say that he concentrated the whole system of English justice round a court of judges professionally expert in the law. He could thus win money— in the Middle Ages no one did justice for nothing— and he could thus win power; he could control, and he could starve, the courts of the feudatories. In offering the nation his royal justice, he offered a strong and sound commodity. Very soon we find very small people—yeomen, peasants—giving the go-by to the old local courts and making their way to Westminster Hall, to plead there about their petty affairs.[1] We may allow that in course of time this concentrating process went much too far. In Edward I.'s day the competence of the local courts in civil causes was hemmed within a limit of forty shillings, a limit which at first was fairly wide, but

[1] The reasons for this suppression of the local courts (and the gradual concentration of justice in the royal courts) are to be found in the superior and even justice administered by the royal courts. This may be illustrated from a detailed study of the three following most important points: the introduction of a new method of procedure by the use of writs and of trial by jury; the regulative influence of the Itinerant Justices; and the protection afforded by the establishment of the three Courts of Common Law at Westminster.— See Medley, *Eng. Consti. Hist.*, 316-32.

became ever narrower as the value of money fell, until in the eighteenth century no one could exact any debt that was not of trifling amount without bringing a costly action in one of the courts at Westminster. But the first stages of the process did unmixed good—they gave us a common law.

King Henry and his able ministers came just in time—a little later would have been too late: English law would have been unified, but it would have been Romanized. We have been wont to boast, perhaps too loudly, of the pure "Englishry" of our common law. This has not been all pure gain. Had we "received" the Roman jurisprudence as our neighbours received it, we should have kept out of many a bad mess through which we have plunged. But to say nothing of the political side of the matter, of the absolute monarchy which Roman law has been apt to bring in its train, it is probably well for us and for the world at large that we have stumbled forwards in our empirical fashion, blundering into wisdom. The moral glow known to the virtuous schoolboy who has not used the "crib" that was ready to his hand, we may allow ourselves to feel; and we may hope for the blessing which awaits all those who have honestly taught themselves anything.

Roman Law in Mediæval Europe. In a few words we must try to tell a long story. On the Continent of Europe Roman law had never perished. After the barbarian invasions it was still the "personal law" of the conquered provincials. The Franks, Lombards, and other victorious tribes lived under their old Germanic customs, while the vanquished lived under the Roman law. In course of time the personal law of the bulk of the inhabitants became the territorial law of the country where they lived. The Roman law became once more the general law of Italy and of Southern France; but in so doing it lost its purity, it became a debased and vulgarized Roman law, to be found rather in traditional custom than in the classical texts, of which very little was known. Then, at the beginning of the twelfth century, came a great change. A law school at Bologna[1] began to study and to teach that Digest in which Justinian had preserved the wisdom of the great jurists of the golden age. A new science spread outwards from Bologna. At least wherever the power of the emperor extended, Roman law had— so men thought—a claim to rule. The emperors, though now of German race, were still the Roman emperors, and the laws of their ancestors were to be found in Justinian's books. But further, the newly discovered system—for we may without much untruth say that it was newly discovered—seemed so reasonable that it could not but affect the develop-

[1] For description of this law school, see Rashdell, *Universities of Europe in the Middle Ages*, I., ch. iv.

ment of law in countries, such as France and England, which paid no obedience to the emperors.

Canon Law. And just at this time a second great system of cosmopolitan jurisprudence was taking shape. For centuries past the Catholic Church had been slowly acquiring a field of jurisdiction that was to be all her own, and for the use of the ecclesiastical tribunals a large body of law had come into being, consisting of the canons published by Church councils and the decretal epistles—genuine and forged—of the popes. Various collections of these were current, but in the middle of the twelfth century they were superseded by the work of Gratian, a monk of Bologna. He called it "The Concordance of Discordant Canons," but it soon became known everywhere as the "Decretum." And by this time the popes were ever busy in pouring out decretal letters, sending them into all corners of the western world. Authoritative collections of these "decretals" were published, and the ecclesiastical lawyer (the "canonist" or "decretist") soon had at his command a large mass of written law comparable to that which the Roman lawyer (the "civilian" or "legist") was studying. A Corpus Juris Canonici begins to take its place beside the Corpus Juris Civilis. Very often the same man had studied both; he was a "doctor of both laws"; and, indeed, the newer system had borrowed largely from the older; it had borrowed its form, its spirit, and a good deal of its matter also.

The canonical jurisprudence of the Italian doctors became the ecclesiastical law of the western world. From all local courts, wherever they might be, there was an appeal to the ultimate tribunal at Rome. But the temporal law of every country felt the influence of the new learning. Apparently we might lay down some such rule as this—that where the attack is longest postponed, it is most severe. In the thirteenth century the Parliament of Paris began the work of harmonizing and rationalizing the provincial customs of Northern France, and this it did by Romanizing them. In the sixteenth century, after the "revival of letters," the Italian jurisprudence took hold of Germany, and swept large portions of the old national law before it. Wherever it finds a weak, because an uncentralized, system of justice, it wins an easy triumph. To Scotland it came late; but it came to stay.[1]

Roman Law in England. To England it came early. Very few are the universities which can boast

[1] "In Scotland it (Roman law) was adopted at the foundation of the Court of Session (1532), on the model of the Parlement of Paris, by King James the Fifth. Political antagonism to England and political attraction to France, together with the influence of the Canonists, naturally determined the King and the Court to follow the system which prevailed on the European continent."—Bryce, *Studies in History and Juris.*, 91. See also P. and M., *Hist. of Eng. Law*, I., 222–4.

of a school of Roman law so old as that of Oxford. In the troubled days of our King Stephen, when the Church was urging new claims against the feeble State, Archbishop Theobald imported from Italy one Vacarius, a Lombard lawyer, who lectured here on Roman law, and wrote a big book that may still be read. Very soon after this Oxford had a flourishing school of civil and canon law. Ever since William the Conqueror had solemnly sanctioned the institution of special ecclesiastical courts, it had been plain that in those courts the law of a Catholic Church, not of a merely English Church, must prevail; also that this law would be in the main Italian law. In the next century, as all know, Henry and Becket fell out as to the definition of the province that was to be left to the ecclesiastical courts. The battle was drawn; neither combatant had gained all that he wanted. Thenceforward until the Protestant Reformation, and indeed until later than that, a border warfare between the two sets of courts was always simmering. Victory naturally inclined to those tribunals which had an immediate control of physical force, but still the sphere that was left to the canonists will seem to our eyes very ample. It comprehended not only the enforcement of ecclesiastical discipline, and the punishment—by spiritual censure, and, in the last resort, by excommunication—of sins left unpunished by temporal law, but also the whole topic of marriage and divorce, those last dying wills and testaments which were closely connected with dying confessions, and the administration of the goods of intestates. Why to this day do we couple "Probate" with "Divorce"? Because in the Middle Ages both of these matters belonged to the "courts Christian." Why to "Probate" and "Divorce" do we add "Admiralty"? Because the civilians— and in England the same man was usually both canonist and civilian—succeeded, though at a comparatively late time, in taking to themselves the litigation that concerned things done on the high seas, those high seas whence no jury could be summoned. So for the canonist there was plenty of room in England; and there was some room for the civilian: he was very useful as a diplomatist.

But we were speaking of our English common law, the law of our ordinary temporal courts, and of the influence upon it of the new Italian but cosmopolitan jurisprudence; and we must confess that for a short while, from the middle of the twelfth to the middle of the thirteenth century, this influence was powerful. The amount of foreign law that was actually borrowed has been underrated and overrated; we could not estimate it without descending to details. Some great maxims and a few more concrete rules were appropriated, but on the whole what was taken was logic, method, spirit, rather than matter.

Glanvill. We may see the effect of this influence very plainly in a Treatise on the Laws of England which comes to us from the last years of Henry II. It has been ascribed to Henry's Chief Justiciar—Viceroy, we may say—Ranulf Glanvill,[1] and whether or no it comes from his pen (he was a layman and a warrior), it describes the practice of the court over which he presided. There are very few sentences in it which we can trace to any Roman book, and yet in a sense the whole book is Roman. We look back from it to a law book written in Henry I.'s time, and we can hardly believe that only some seventy years divide the two. The one can at this moment be read and understood by any one who knows a little of mediæval Latin and a little of English law; the other will always be dark to the most learned scholars. The gulf between them looks like that between logic and caprice, between reason and unreason.

Bracton. And then from the middle of the thirteenth century we have a much greater and better book than Glanvill's. Its author we know as Bracton, though his name really was Henry of Bratton.[2]

---

[1] Translation of Glanvill, by John Beames, London, 1812. Reprinted, with Introduction, by J. H. Beale, Jr., Washington, D. C., 1901.

For description of this commentary of Glanvill, the first systematic Treatise on English Law, see P. & M., *Hist. of Eng. Law*, I., 162–67; Holdsworth, *Hist. of Eng. Law*, II., 146–60.

[2] Bracton, *De Legibus et Consuetudinibus Angliæ*, edited, with notes, by Sir Travers Twiss, 6 vols., London, 1878–83. For description of

He was an ecclesiastic, an archdeacon, but for many years he was one of the king's justices. He had read a great deal of the Italian jurisprudence, chiefly in the works of that famous doctor, Azo of Bologna. Thence he had obtained his idea of what a law book should be, of how law should be arranged and stated; thence also he borrowed maxims and some concrete rules; with these he can fill up the gaps in our English system. But he lets us see that not much more can now be done in the way of romanization.   Ever since Henry II.'s time the king's court has been hard at work amassing precedents, devising writs, and commenting upon them.   Bracton himself has laboriously collected five hundred decisions from the mile-long rolls of the court and uses them as his authorities.[1] For him English law is already "case

this book, "the crown and flower of English mediæval jurisprudence," see P. and M., I., 206–09, and Holdsworth, *Hist. of Eng. Law*, II., 185–235.

[1] "The book now known as Bracton's *Note Book* and edited by Mr. F. W. Maitland (3 vols., London, 1887), may perhaps fairly be reckoned a book of reports. If so, we may claim for Bracton, under whose direction and for whose use it was almost certainly compiled, the honour of having been the first of our reporters as well as the first methodical English text-writer. The contents of this book 'may be briefly described as transcripts of entries on the judicial rolls of the first twenty-four years of Henry III.,' that is, from A.D. 1218 onwards. Entries of this early period give us, for reasons which are part of the substantive history of the law, much fuller information as to what really happened in court than the more elaborate and formal pleadings of the later common-law system. The only thing which need make us hesitate to call the *Note Book* a book of reports is the

law"; a judgment is a precedent. While as yet the science of the civilians was a somewhat unpractical science, while as yet they had not succeeded in bringing the old classical texts into close contact with the facts of mediæval life, the king's court of professional justices—the like of which was hardly to be found in any foreign land, in any unconquered land—had been rapidly evolving a common law for England, establishing a strict and formal routine of procedure, and tying the hands of all subsequent judges. From Bracton's day onwards Roman law exercises but the slightest influence on the English common law, and such influence as it exercises is rather by way of repulsion than by way of attraction. English law at this early period had absorbed so much Romanism that it could withstand all future attacks, and pass scathless even through the critical sixteenth century.

It may be convenient, however, to pause at this point in the development of our judicial institutions, in order to trace the history of our legal procedure.

History of Trial by Jury. For a long time past Englishmen have been proud of their trial by jury,

---

absence of any indication that it was meant to be communicated to the profession in general, or used by Bracton himself otherwise than as material for his treatise on the laws of England. It is really half-way between reporting and the 'common placing' of later times. Much later, and in a roundabout fashion, part of the matter contained in the *Note Book* passed into English legal literature."— Pollock, *First Book of Juris.*, 277–8.

proud to see the nations of Europe imitating as best they might this "palladium of English liberties," this "bulwark of the British Constitution." Their pride, if in other respects it be reasonable, need not be diminished by any modern discoveries of ancient facts, even though they may have to learn that in its origin trial by jury was rather French than English, rather royal than popular, rather the livery of conquest than a badge of freedom. They have made it what it is; and what it is is very different from what it was. The story is a long and a curious one.

Legal Forms in the Twelfth Century. Let us try to put before our eyes a court of the twelfth century; it may be a county court, or a hundred-court, or a court held by some great baron for his tenants. It is held in the open air—perhaps upon some ancient moot-hill, which ever since the times of heathenry has been the scene of justice. An officer presides over it—the sheriff, the sheriff's bailiff, the lord's steward. But all or many of the free landowners of the district are bound to attend it; they owe "suit" to it, they are its suitors, they are its doomsmen; it is for them, and not for the president, "to find the dooms." He controls the procedure, he issues the mandates, he pronounces the sentence; but when the question is what the judgment shall be, he bids the suitors find a doom. All this is very ancient, and look where we will in Western Europe we may find it. But as yet we have not found the germ of trial by jury. These doomsmen are not "judges of fact." There is no room for any judges of fact. If of two litigants the one contradicts the other flatly, if the plain "You did" of the one is met by the straightforward "You lie" of the other, here is a problem that man cannot solve. He is unable as yet to weigh testimony against testimony, to cross-examine witnesses, to piece together the truth out of little bits of evidence. He has recourse to the supernatural. He adjudges that one or other of the two parties is to prove his case by an appeal to God.

The Oath. The judgment precedes the proof. The proof consists, not in a successful attempt to convince your judges of the truth of your assertion, but in the performance of a task that they have imposed upon you: if you perform it, God is on your side. The modes of proof are two, oaths and ordeals. In some cases we may see a defendant allowed to swear away a charge by his own oath. More frequently he will have to bring with him oath-helpers—in later days they are called "compurgators"—and when he has sworn successfully, each of these oath-helpers in turn will swear "By God that oath is clean and true." The doomsmen have decreed how many oath-helpers, and of what quality, he must bring. A great deal of their traditional legal lore consists in rules about this matter; queer arithmetical rules which teach how the oath of one thegn is as weighty as the oaths of six ceorls, and the like. Sometimes they require that the oath-helpers shall be kinsmen of the principal swearer, and so warn us against any rationalism which would turn these oath-helpers into "witnesses to character," and probably tell us of the time when the bond of blood was so strong that a man's kinsfolk were answerable for his misdeeds. A very easy task this oath with oath-helpers may seem in our eyes. It is not so easy as it looks. Ceremonial rules must be strictly observed; a set form of words must be pronounced; a slip, a stammer, will spoil all, and the adversary will win his cause. Besides, it is common knowledge that those who perjure themselves are often struck dead, or reduced to the stature of dwarfs, or find that they cannot remove their hands from the relics that they have profaned.

The Ordeal. But when crime is laid to a man's charge he will not always be allowed to escape with oaths. Very likely he will be sent to the ordeal. The ordeal is conceived as the "judgment of God." Of heathen origin it well may be, but long ago the Christian Church has made it her own, has prescribed a solemn ritual for the consecration of those instruments—the fire, the water—which will reveal the truth. The water in the pit is adjured to receive the innocent and to reject the guilty. He who sinks is safe, he who floats is lost. The red-hot iron one pound in weight must be lifted and carried three paces. The hand that held it is then sealed up in a cloth. Three days afterwards the seal is broken. Is the hand clean or is it foul? that is the dread question. A blister "as large as half a walnut" is fatal. How these tests worked in practice we do not know. We seldom get stories about them save when, as now and again will happen, the local saint interferes and performs a miracle. We cannot but guess that it was well to be good friends with the priest when one went to the ordeal.

Trial by Battle. Then the Norman conquerors brought with them another ordeal—the judicial combat. An ordeal it is, for though the Church has looked askance at it, it is no appeal to mere brute force; it is an appeal to the God of Battles. Very solemnly does each combatant swear to the truth of his cause; very solemnly does he swear that he has eaten nothing, drunk nothing "whereby the law of God may be debased or the devil's law exalted."

When a criminal charge is made—"an appeal of felony"—the accuser and the accused, if they be not maimed, nor too young, nor too old, will have to fight in person. When a claim for land is made, the plaintiff has to offer battle, not in his own person, but in the person of one of his men. This man is in theory a witness who will swear to the justice of his

4

lord's cause. In theory he ought not to be, but in practice he often is, a hired champion who makes a profession of fighting other people's battles. If the hireling be exposed, he may have his hand struck off; but as a matter of fact there were champions in a large way of business. At least in some cases the arms that are used are very curious; they are made of wood and horn, and look (for we have pictures of them) like short pickaxes. Possibly they have been in use for this sacral purpose—a sacral purpose it is— ever since an age which knew not iron. Also we know that the champion's head is shaved, but are left to guess why this is done. The battle may last the livelong day, until the stars appear.

The accuser has undertaken that in the course of a day he will "prove by his body" the truth of his charge; and if he cannot do this before the twilight falls, he has failed and is a perjurer. The object of each party in the fight is not so much to kill his adversary—this perhaps he is hardly likely to do with the archaic weapon that he wields—but to make him pronounce "the loathsome word," to make him cry "craven." In a criminal case the accused, if van- quished, was forthwith hanged or mutilated; but in any case the craven had to pay a fine of sixty shillings, the old "king's ban" of the Frankish laws, and, having in effect confessed himself a perjurer, he was thenceforward infamous.

Growth of King's Courts. But long ago the Frankish kings had placed themselves outside the sphere of this ancient formal and sacral procedure. They were standing in the shoes of Roman governors, even of Roman emperors. For themselves and their own affairs they had a prerogatival procedure. If their rights were in question, they would direct their officers to call together the best and oldest men of the neighbourhood to swear about the relevant facts. The royal officers would make an inquisition, hold an inquest, force men to swear that they would return true answers to whatever questions might be addressed to them in the king's name. They may be asked whether or no this piece of land belongs to the king; they may be asked in a general way what lands the king has in their district; they may be asked (for the king is beginning to see that he has a great interest in the suppression of violent crime) to tell tales of their neighbours, to report the names of all who are suspected of murder or robbery, and then these men can be sent to the ordeal. This privilege that the king has he can concede to others; he can grant to his favourite churches that their lands shall stand outside the scope of the clumsy and hazardous procedure of the common courts; if their title to those lands be challenged, a royal officer will call upon the neighbours to declare the truth—in other words, to give a verdict. It is here that we see the germ of the jury.

The Norman duke in his conquered kingdom was able to use the inquest with a free hand and on a grand scale. Domesday Book was compiled out of the verdicts returned by the men of the various hundreds and townships of England in answer to a string of questions put to them by royal commissioners. We have read how the stern king thought it no shame to do what the English monk thought it shame to write, how he numbered every ox, every cow, every pig in England. Thenceforward the inquest was part of the machinery of government; it could be employed for many different purposes whenever the king desired information. He could use it in his own litigation, he could place it at the service of other litigants who were fortunate enough or rich enough to obtain this favour from him. But throughout the reigns of our Norman kings it keeps its prerogatival character.[1]

[1] "For more than a hundred years after the Conquest the ancient Anglo-Saxon modes of trial, or forms of proof, by ordeal (*judicium Dei*), by oath (compurgation, termed later on 'wager of law'), by witnesses, and by production of charters, continued in general use, side by side with the Norman procedure, the wager of battle—an innovation detested by the English, and at length gladly laid aside by the Normans themselves,—and the occasional use of the Inquest by sworn recognitors. It was only gradually, however, that the advantages of the principle of recognition by jury in its application to judicial procedure became impressed upon the minds of both rulers and ruled. At first the sworn inquest seems to have been chiefly applied to matters not judicial, such as the ascertainment of the laws of King Edward, the Domesday survey, the assessment of feudal taxation under William Rufus and Henry I., and the customs

The King's Assizes. Then Henry II., bent upon making his justice supreme throughout his realm, put this royal remedy at the disposal of all his subjects. This he did not by one general law, but piecemeal, by a series of ordinances known as "assizes," some of which we may yet read, while others have perished. For example, when there was litigation about the ownership of land, the defendant, instead of accepting the plaintiff's challenge to fight, was allowed to "put himself upon the king's grand assize."[1] Thereupon the action, which had been

---

of the church of York, which the latter monarch, in 1106, directed five commissioners to verify by the oath of twelve of the citizens. There are, however, equally early instances of strictly legal matters being decided by the recognition on oath of a certain number of *probi et legales homines*, selected from the men of the county to represent the neighbourhood and testify to facts of which they had special knowledge. . . .

"The use of a jury, both for criminal presentment and civil inquest, is mentioned for the first time in our statute law in the Constitutions of Clarendon (1164). The way in which the jury is therein referred to seems to imply that it had already gone into general use and favour."—Taswell-Langmead, *Eng. Consti. Hist.*, 135–7.

[1] The exact date of the Grand Assize is unknown.

"It is described by Glanvill as a Royal boon conferred on the people, with the counsel and consent of the *proceres*, to relieve freeholders from the hardship of defending the title of their lands by the doubtful issue of trial by battle. By the Grand Assize the defendant was allowed his choice between wager of battle and the recognition (*i. e.*, knowledge) of a jury of twelve sworn knights of the vicinage summoned for that purpose by the sheriff. . . .

"In both cases" (those involving either the ownership or the possession of land) "the recognitors were sworn to found their verdict upon their own knowledge, gained either by eye-witness or by the words of their fathers, or by such words as they were bound to

begun in some feudal court, was removed into the King's court; and twelve knights, chosen from the district in which the land lay, gave a verdict as to whether the plaintiff or the defendant had the better right.

In other cases—for example, when the dispute was about the possession, not the ownership, of land—less solemn forms of the inquest were employed: twelve free and lawful men, not necessarily knights, were charged to say whether the defendant had ejected the plaintiff. Before the twelfth century was at an end, the inquest in one form or another—sometimes it was called an assize, sometimes a jury—had become part of the normal procedure in almost every kind of civil action. Still there long remained many cases in which a defendant could, if he chose, reject the new-fangled mode of trial, and claim the ancient right of purging himself with oath-helpers, or of picking up the glove that the plaintiff had thrown down as a gage of battle. Even a prelate of the Church would sometimes rely rather upon the strong

---

have as much confidence in as if they were their own. The proceeding by assize was in fact merely the sworn testimony of a certain number of persons summoned to give evidence upon matters within their own knowledge. They were themselves the only witnesses. If all were ignorant of the facts a fresh jury had to be summoned; if some of them only were ignorant, or if they could not agree, others were to be added—a process subsequently called *afforcing* the jury— until a verdict could be obtained from twelve unanimous witnesses."
—Taswell-Langmead, *Eng. Consti. Hist.*, 137–8.

arm of a professional pugilist than upon the testimony of his neighbours.

Within the walls of the chartered boroughs men were conservative of all that would favour the free burgher at the cost of the despised outsider. The Londoners thought that trial by jury was good enough for those who were not citizens, but the citizen must be allowed to swear away charges of debt or trespass by the oaths of his friends. In the old communal courts, too, the county and hundred courts, where the landowners of the district sat as doomsmen, trial by jury never struck root, for only by virtue of a royal writ could a jury be summoned: this is one of the reasons why those old courts languished, decayed, and became useless. However, before the Middle Ages were over, trial by jury had become the only form of trial for civil actions that had any vitality. So late as 1824[1] a lucky litigant, taking advantage of his adversary's slip, presented himself at the bar of the King's Bench, prepared to swear away a debt—"to make his law" was the technical phrase—with the aid of eleven oath-helpers, and not until 1833[2] was this world-old procedure abolished by statute; but long before this, if the plaintiff was well-advised, he could

[1] King vs. Williams, 2 B. &. C. 538; Thayer, *Evidence at Common Law*, 33.

[2] 3 & 4 Wm. IV., c. 42, s. 13.

always prevent his opponent from escaping in this easy fashion.

The Earliest Jury-Trial. We have spoken of "trial by jury." That term naturally calls up before our minds a set of twelve men called into court in order that they may listen to the testimony of witnesses, give a true verdict "according to the evidence," and, in short, act as judges of those questions of fact that are in dispute. But it is very long after Henry II.'s day before trial by jury takes this form. Originally the jurors are called in, not in order that they may hear, but in order that they may give, evidence. They are witnesses. They are the neighbours of the parties; they are presumed to know before they come into court the facts about which they are to testify. They are chosen by the sheriff to represent the neighbourhood—indeed, they are spoken of as being "the neighbourhood," "the country"—and the neighbourhood, the country will know the facts.

In the twelfth century population was sparse, and men really knew far more of the doings of their neighbours than we know nowadays. It was expected that all legal transactions would take place in public; the conveyance of land was made in open court, the wife was endowed at the church-door, the man who bought cattle in secret ran a great but just risk of being treated as a thief[1]; every three weeks a

[1] See Market Overt, Blackstone, *Com.*, II., 449–50.

court was held in the village, and all the affairs of
every villager were discussed. The verdict, then,
was the sworn testimony of the countryside; and if
the twelve jurors perjured themselves, the verdict
of another jury of twenty-four might send them to
prison and render them infamous for ever.[1]

In course of time, and by slow degrees—degrees
so slow that we can hardly detect them—the jury
put off its old and acquired a new character. Sometimes, when the jurors knew nothing of the facts,
witnesses who did know the facts would be called
in to supply the requisite information. As human
affairs grew more complex, the neighbours whom the
sheriff summoned became less and less able to perform their original duty, more and more dependent
upon the evidence given in their presence by those
witnesses who were summoned by the parties. In
the fifteenth century the change had taken place,
though in yet later days a man who had been summoned as a juror, and who sought to escape on the
ground that he already knew something of the facts
in question, would be told that he had given a very
good reason for his being placed in the jury-box.

---

[1] For description of writ of attaint and result of verdict by jury
of twenty-four, see P. and M., *Hist. of Eng. Law*, II., 541-3 and
665; Thayer, *Prelim. Treatise on Evidence*, 137-9, and index; Blackstone, *Com.*, III., 402-5; Stephen, *Hist. of Crim. Law of Eng.*, I.,
306-7; Taswell-Langmead, *Eng. Consti. Hist.*, 141-2; Medley, *Eng.
Consti. Hist.*, 410-11.

We may well say, therefore, that trial by jury, though it has its roots in the Frankish inquest, grew up on English soil; and until recent times it was distinctive of England and Scotland, for on the Continent of Europe all other forms of legal procedure had been gradually supplanted by that which canonists and civilians had constructed out of ancient Roman elements.

Criminal Procedure. We have yet to speak of the employment of the inquest in criminal cases. The Frankish kings had employed it for the purpose of detecting crime. Do you suspect any of murder, robbery, larceny, or the like? This question was addressed by royal officers to selected representatives of every neighbourhood, and answered upon oath, and the suspected persons were sent to "the judgment of God." The Church borrowed this procedure; the bishop could detect ecclesiastical offences as the king detected crimes.

It is not impossible that this particular form of the inquest had made its way into England some half-century before the Norman Conquest; but we hear very little about it until the days of Henry II. He ordained that it should be used upon a very large scale and as a matter of ordinary practice, both by the justices whom he sent to visit the counties and by the sheriffs. From his time onward a statement made upon oath by a set of jurors representing a

hundred, to the effect that such an one is suspected
of such a crime, is sufficient to put a man upon his
trial. It is known as an indictment. It takes its
place beside the old accusation, or "appeal," urged
by the person who has been wronged, by the man
whose goods have been stolen, or the nearest kinsman
of the murdered man. It is but an accusation, however, and in Henry's days the indicted person takes
his chance at the hot iron or the cold water; God
may be for him, though man be against him. But
already some suspicion is shown of the so-called
judgment of God; for though he comes clean from the
ordeal, he has to leave the country, swearing never
to return.

At last, in 1215, the Fourth Lateran Council forbade the clergy to take part in this superstitious
rite. After this we hear no more in England of the
ordeal as a legal process, though in much later days
the popular belief that witches will swim died hard,
and many an old woman was put in the pond. The
judges of the thirteenth century had no substitute
ready to take the place of that supernatural test of
which an enlightened Pope (Innocent III.) had deprived them. Of course if the indicted person will
agree to accept the verdict of his neighbours, will
"put himself upon his country"—that is, upon the
neighbourhood—for good and ill, all is easy. Those
who have indicted him as a suspicious character can

now be asked whether he is guilty or no; and if they say that he is guilty, there will be no harm in hanging him, for he consented to the trial, and he must abide the consequences. To make the trial yet fairer, one may call in a second jury different from that which indicted him.

Here is the origin of those two juries which we see employed in our own days—the grand jury that indicts, and the petit jury that tries. But suppose that he will not give his consent; it is by no means obvious that the testimony of his neighbours ought to be treated as conclusive. Hitherto he has been able to invoke the judgment of God, and can we now deprive him of this ancient, this natural right?

Peine Forte et Dure. No, no one can be tried by jury who does not consent to be so tried. But what we can do is this—we can compel him to give his consent, we can starve him into giving his consent, and, again, we can quicken the slow action of starvation by laying him out naked on the floor of the dungeon and heaping weights upon his chest until he says that he will abide by the verdict of his fellows. And so we are brought to the pedantic cruelty of the *peine forte et dure.*[1] Even in the seventeenth century there were men who would endure the

---

[1] For the development of this punishment, see P. and M., *Hist. of Eng. Law,* II., 651–2; Thayer, *Prelim. Treatise on Evidence,* 74–81; Stephen, *Hist. of Crim. Law of Eng.,* I., 298; Taswell-Langmead, *Eng. Consti. Hist.,* 139, and note.

agony of being pressed to death rather than utter the
few words which would have subjected them to a
trial by jury. They had a reason for their fortitude.
Had they been hanged as felons their property would
have been confiscated, their children would have
been penniless; while, as it was, they left the world
obstinate indeed, but unconvicted. All this—and
until 1772[1] men might still be pressed to death—
takes us back to a time when the ordeal seems the
fair and natural mode of ascertaining guilt and
innocence, when the jury is still a new-fangled
institution.

The indictment, we have said, took its place
beside the "appeal"—the old private accusation.
The owner of the stolen goods, the kinsman of the
murdered man, might still prosecute his suit in the
old manner, and offer to prove his assertions by his
body. The Church had not abolished, and could not
abolish, the judicial combat, for though in truth it
was an ordeal, no priestly benediction of the instruments that were to be used was necessary. By
slow degrees in the thirteenth century the accused
acquired the right of refusing his accuser's challenge
and of putting himself upon a jury. What is more,
the judges began to favour the "indictment" and to
discourage the "appeal" by all possible means.
They required of the accuser a punctilious obser-

[1] 12 Geo. III., c. 20.

vance of ancient formalities, and would quash his accusation if he were guilty of the smallest blunder.

Still, throughout the Middle Ages we occasionally hear of battles being fought over criminal cases. In particular a convicted felon would sometimes turn "approver"—that is to say, he would obtain a pardon conditional on his ridding the world, by means of his appeals, of some three or four other felons. If he failed in his endeavour, he was forthwith hanged. But those who were not antiquarians must have long ago ceased to believe that such a barbarism as trial by battle was possible, when in 1818 a case arose which showed them that they had inadequately gauged the dense conservatism of the laws of their country.

Abraham Thornton's Case, 1818. One Mary Ashford was found drowned; one Abraham Thornton was indicted for murdering her; a jury acquitted him. But the verdict did not satisfy the public mind, and the brother of the dead girl had recourse to an "appeal": to this accusation the previous acquittal was no answer.[1] Thornton declared himself ready

---

[1] "The origin of this private process for the punishment of public crimes was doubtless derived from the old days when a *wergild* was payable to the relatives of the slain. . . .

"If the appellee was worsted in the combat, or found guilty, he suffered the same judgment as if convicted on an indictment, but the Crown had no power to pardon him, because an 'appeal' was a private suit.

"From the date of the Statute 3 Hen. VII., ch. i., an appeal might

to defend his innocence by his body, and threw down in Westminster Hall, as his gage of battle, an antique gauntlet, "without either fingers or thumb, made of white tanned skin, ornamented with sewn tracery and silk fringes, crossed by a narrow band of red leather, with leathern tags and thongs for fastening." The judges did their best to discover some slip in his procedure; but he had been careful and well advised; even his glove was of the true mediæval pattern. So there was nothing for it but to declare that he was within his rights, and could not be compelled to submit to a jury if he preferred to fight. His adversary had no mind to fight, and so let the glove alone. After this crowning scandal Parliament at last bestirred itself, and in the year of grace 1819 completed the work of Pope Innocent III. by abolishing the last of the ordeals.[1]

The Working of Trial by Jury. If we regard it as an engine for the discovery of truth and for the punishment of malefactors, the mediæval jury was a clumsy thing. Too often its verdicts must have represented guess-work and the tittle-tattle of the

---

be brought even after the appellee had been tried and acquitted on an indictment. The 'Battel' took place in the presence of the Judges of the Court of Common Pleas, attired in the scarlet robes, who sat looking on while the combatants, each armed with a staff an ell long and a leathern shield, cudgelled each other from sunrise to starrising, or until one of them cried, 'craven.'"—Taswell-Langmead, *Eng. Consti. Hist.*, 103–4.

[1] Passed, June 22, 1819. 59 Geo. III., c. 46.

countryside. Sometimes a man must have gone to
the gallows, not because any one had seen him commit
a crime, not because guilt had been brought home to
him by a carefully tested chain of proved facts, but
because it was notorious that he was just the man
from whom a murder or a robbery might be expected.
Only by slow degrees did the judges insist that the
jurors ought to listen to evidence given by witnesses
in open court, and rely only upon the evidence that
was there given.[1] Even when this step had been
taken, it was long before our modern law of evidence
took shape, long before the judges laid down such
rules as that "hearsay is not evidence," and that
testimony which might show that the prisoner had
committed other crimes was not relevant to the
question whether he had perpetrated the particular
offence of which he stood indicted.

But whatever may have been the case in the days
of the ordeal—and about this we know very little—
we may be fairly certain that in the later Middle
Ages the escape of the guilty was far commoner than

---

[1] "Early in the reign of Henry IV. a further advance was made.
All evidence was required to be given at the bar of the court, so that
the Judges might be enabled to exclude improper testimony.
"From this change flowed two important consequences:
"(1) From the exercise of control on the part of the Judges sprang
up the whole system of rules as to Evidence.
"(2) The practice of receiving evidence openly at the bar of the
Court produced a great extension of the duty of an advocate."
—Taswell-Langmead, *Eng. Consti. Hist.*, 141.

the punishment of the guiltless. After some hesitation our law had adopted its well-known rule that a jury can give no verdict unless the twelve men are all of one mind.[1] To obtain a condemnatory unanimity was not easy if the accused was a man of good family; one out of every twelve of his neighbours that might be taken at random would stand out loyally for his innocence. Bribery could do much; seignorial influence could do more; the sheriff, who was not incorruptible, and had his own likes and dislikes, could do all, since it was for him to find the jury.

It is easy for us to denounce as unconstitutional the practice which prevailed under Tudors and Stuarts of making jurors answer for their verdicts before the King's Council[2]; it is not so easy for us to make certain

---

[1] "The number of the recognitors was at first undefined, but when Glanvill wrote, under Henry II., twelve appears to have been the usual, though not the invariable, number mentioned in the King's writs. We have seen that it was necessary that twelve jurymen should concur in their verdict, and this result, in civil cases at least, was procured by 'afforcing' the jury, that is, adding other recognitors from the vicinage who were acquainted with the matter. But the difficulty of procuring a verdict of twelve caused for a time the verdict of a majority to be received. In the reign of Edward III., however, the necessity for a unanimous verdict of twelve was re-established."—Taswell-Langmead, *Eng. Consti. Hist.*, 140. For fuller treatment see Thayer, *Evidence at Common Law*, 86–90.

[2] For liability of juries to fine and imprisonment by Star Chamber see Throckmorton's Case, State Trials, 869.

"After the abolition of the Star Chamber (1641) the Crown made use of the Judges to intimidate Juries. At length the immunity of Juries was finally established in 1670 by the celebrated decision of Chief Justice Vaughan in *Bushell's Case* (6 State Trials, 999)."—Taswell-Langmead, *Eng. Consti. Hist.*, 142.

5

that the jury system would have lived through the 16th century had it not been for the action of this somewhat irregular check. For the rest, we may notice that the jury of the Middle Ages, if it is to be called a democratic institution, can be called so only in a mediæval sense. The jurors were freeholders; the great mass of Englishmen were not freeholders. The peasant who was charged with a crime was acquitted or convicted by the word of his neighbours, but by the word of neighbours who considered themselves very much his superiors.

If, however, we look back to these old days, we shall find ourselves deploring, not so much that some men of whose guilt we are by no means satisfied are sent to the gallows, as that many men whose guilt is but too obvious escape scot-free. We take up a roll upon which the presentments of the jurors are recorded. Everywhere the same tale meets our eye: "Malefactors came by night to the house of such an one at such a place; they slew him and his wife and his sons and his daughters, and robbed his house; we do not know who they were; we suspect no one."

Such organization as there was for the pursuit of these marauders was utterly inefficient. Every good and lawful man is bound to follow the hue and cry[1]

---

[1] The early police organization of England was elaborated and completed by the Statute of Winchester, 13 Edward I., 1285. For its text, see Stubbs, *Select Charters*, 469–74. For summary of its provisions, see Taswell-Langmead, *Eng. Consti. Hist.*, 159, and Jenks, *Edward I.*, 220–22.

when it is raised, and the village reeve, or in later
days the village constable, ought to put himself at
the head of this improvised and unprofessional police
force. But it was improvised and unprofessional.
Outside the walls of the boroughs there was no regular plan of watch and ward, no one whose business
it was to keep an eye on men of suspicious habits, or
to weave the stray threads of evidence into a halter.
The neighbours who had followed the trail of the
stolen cattle to the county boundary were apt to turn
back, every man to his plough. "Let Gloucestershire
folk mind Gloucestershire rogues." They would be
fined and amerced, when the justices came round, for
neglect of their duties—for the sheriff, or the coroner,
or some one else, would tell tales of them—but meanwhile their hay was about, and the weather was rainy.
Even when the jurors know the criminal's name, the
chances seem to be quite ten to one that he has not
been captured. Nothing could then be done but
outlaw him. At four successive county courts—the
county court was held month by month—a proclamation calling upon him to present himself, "to come into the King's Peace,"[1] would be made, and at the

[1] "In later times the King's Peace became a synonym for public
order maintained by the King's general authority; nowadays we do
not easily conceive how the peace which lawful men ought to keep
can be any other than the Queen's or the commonwealth's. But the
King's justice, as we have seen, was at first not ordinary but exceptional, and his power was called to aid only when other means had
failed. To be in the King's Peace was to have a special protection, a

fifth court he would be declared an outlaw. If after this he were caught, then, unless he could obtain some favour from the king, he would be condemned to death without any investigation being made of his guilt or innocence; the mere fact of his outlawry being proved, sentence followed as a matter of course. But the old law had been severer than this: to slay the outlaw wherever he might be found was not only the right but the duty of every true man, and even in the middle of the thirteenth century this was still the customary law of the Welsh marches.

The outlaw of real life was not the picturesque figure that we have seen upon the stage; if he and his men were really "merry" in the greenwood, they were merry in creditable circumstances. Still, it is

---

local or personal privilege. Every free man was entitled to peace in his own house, the sanctity of the homestead being one of the most ancient and general principles of Teutonic law. The worth set on a man's peace, like that of his life, varied with his rank, and thus the king's peace was higher than any other man's. Fighting in the King's house was a capital offence from an early time. Gradually the privileges of the King's house were extended to the precincts of his court, to the army, to the regular meetings of the shire and hundred, and to the great roads. Also the King might grant special personal protection to his officers and followers; and these two kinds of privilege spread until they coalesced and covered the whole ground." Pollock, "Eng. Law before the Nor. Conquest," *Law Quar. Review*, XIV., 301.

For further description of the King's Peace and the process by which it was established, see Pollock, *Oxford Lectures and other Discourses*, ch. iii.; P. and M., *Hist. of Eng. Law*, I., 44–5; Pollock, "King's Peace in Middle Ages," *Harv. Law Rev.*, XIII. (1900), 177–89, reprinted in *Anglo-Am. Legal Hist.*, II., ch. xxxii.

not to be denied that he attracted at times a good deal of romantic sympathy, even in the ages which really knew him. This probably had its origin in the brutal stringency of the forest laws, which must be charged with the stupid blunder of punishing small offences with a rigour which should have been reserved for the worst crimes.

The worst crimes were common enough. Every now and then the king and the nation would be alarmed, nor needlessly alarmed, by the prevalence of murder and highway robbery. A new ordinance would be issued, new instructions would be given to the judges, sheriffs would be active, and jurors would be eager to convict; a good deal of hanging would be done, perhaps too indiscriminately. But so soon as the panic was over, Justice would settle down into her old sluggish habits. Throughout the Middle Ages life was very insecure; there was a great deal of nocturnal marauding, and the knife that every Englishman wore was apt to stab upon slight provocation.

The Right of Sanctuary. The Church had not mended matters by sanctifying places and persons. In very old days when the blood-feud raged, when punishment and vengeance were very much one, it was a good thing that there should be holy places to which a man might flee when the avenger of blood was behind—places where no drop of blood might be spilt without sacrilege. They afforded an opportunity for the peacemaker. The bishop or priest would not yield up the fugitive who lay panting at the foot of the altar until terms had been made between him and his pursuers. But at a later time when the State was endeavouring to punish criminals, and there would be no punishment until after trial, the sanctuary was a public nuisance.

The law was this: If a criminal entered a church he was safe from pursuit; the neighbours who were pursuing him were bound to beset the church, prevent his escape, and send for the coroner. Sometimes they would remain encamped round the church for many days. At last the coroner would come, and parley with the fugitive. If he confessed his crime, then he might "abjure the realm"—that is, swear to leave England within a certain number of days (he was allowed days enough to enable him to reach the nearest seaport), and never to return. If he strayed from the straight road which led to the haven, or if he came back to the realm, then he could at once be sentenced to death. For a man to take sanctuary, confess his crime, and abjure the realm, was an everyday event, and we must have thus shipped off many a malefactor to plunder our neighbours in France and Flanders. If the man who had taken sanctuary would neither confess to a crime, nor submit to a trial, the State could do no more against him. It tried to teach the clergy that their duty was to starve him into submission; but the clergy resented this interference with holy things. A bad element of caprice was introduced into the administration of justice. The strong, the swift, the premeditating murderer cheated the gallows. Especially in the towns he might fairly complain of bad luck if he could not slip into one of the numerous churches before he was caught. On the other hand, the man who had not plotted his crime would get hanged.

Benefit of Clergy. And then the clergy stood outside the criminal law. If a clerk in holy orders committed a crime—this was the law of the thirteenth century—he could not be tried for it in a lay court. He could be accused there, and the judges might ask a jury whether he was guilty or no; but even though they found him guilty, this was no trial. At the request of his bishop—and the bishops made such requests as a matter of course—he was handed over for trial in an ecclesiastical court. Such a court had power to inflict very heavy punishments. It might draw no drop of blood, but it could imprison for life, besides being able to degrade the clerk from his orders. As a matter of fact, however, we hear very little of any punishment save that of degradation. What is more, the criminal procedure of the ecclesiastical courts in England was of an absurdly old-fashioned and clumsy kind. They held by compurgation. If the accused clerk could but get some eleven or twelve friends of his own profession to swear that they believed him innocent, he was acquitted; he might resume his criminal career. Church and State were both to blame for this sad story. The Church would yield no jot of the claims that were sanctified by the blood of St. Thomas; the lay courts would not suffer the bishops to do criminal justice in a really serious fashion. There can be no doubt that many of the worst criminals—men who had been found guilty by a jury of brutal murders and rapes—escaped scot-free, because they had about them some slight savour of professional holiness. It should be understood that this immunity was shared with the bishops, priests, and deacons by a vast multitude of men who were in "minor orders." They might have no ecclesiastical duties to perform; they might be married; they might be living the same life which laymen lived; but they stood outside the ordinary criminal law.

One of the worst evils of the later Middle Ages was this benefit of clergy. The king's justices, who never loved it, at length reduced it to an illogical absurdity. They would not be at pains to require any real proof of a prisoner's sacred character. If he could read a line in a book, this would do; indeed, it is even said that the same verse of the Psalms was set before the eyes of every prisoner, so that even the illiterate might escape if he could repeat by heart those saving words. Criminal law had been rough and rude, and sometimes cruel; it had used the gallows too readily; it had punished with death thefts which, owing to a great fall in the value of money, were becoming petty thefts. Still, cruelty in such matters is better than caprice, and the benefit of clergy[1] had made the law capricious without making it less cruel.

[1] A privilege of exemption from capital punishment granted to all who could read. The prisoner was then handed over to the Court Christian, where he cleared himself upon his oath and that of persons as his compurgators. Later, it could be claimed by laymen only once; and they were burned in the hand. The privilege only applied to capital felonies, and was abolished in 1827, by Geo. IV., c. 28. s. 6, 7-8.

READINGS

On Domesday Book:
Maitland, *Domesday and Beyond*, Essay 1; Pollock, "A Brief Survey of Domesday," *Eng. Hist. Rev.*, 1896, 209–30; Freeman, *Nor. Conquest*, V., ch. xxii., and appendix; Ellis, H., "General Introduction to Domesday Book," *Record Com.*, London, 1833; Holdsworth, *Hist. of Eng. Law*, II., 24, and 118–29; Taswell-Langmead, *Eng. Consti. Hist.*, ch. ii., 46–7.

On Preservation of Old English Law under Norman Kings and their Legislation:
P. and M., *Hist. of Eng. Law*, I., 88–107; Taswell-Langmead, *Eng. Consti. Hist.*, chaps. ii. and iii.

On our Legal Language:
P. and M., *Hist. of Eng. Law*, I., 80–5; Holdsworth, *Hist. of Eng. Law*, II., 397–402.

On Legal Reforms of Henry II.:
P. and M., *Hist. of Eng. Law*, I., 136–56; Holdsworth, *Hist. of Eng. Law*, I., 26–36, and II., 137–65; Carter, *Hist. Eng. Legal Insti.*, chaps. vii., viii., ix.; Green, Mrs. J. R., *Henry the Second*, chaps. iii., iv., v., and ix., reprinted in *Anglo-Am. Legal Hist.*, I., ch. iv.; Taswell-Langmead, *Eng. Consti. Hist.*, 129–38.

On Roman Law in Mediæval Europe:
Hunter, W. A., *Hist. Roman Law*, 90–3, 98–116; Hadley, *Introduction to Roman Law*, ch. ii.; Morey, *Outlines of Roman Law*, 167–91, Period 5, chaps. i., ii.

On Canon Law in England:
Stubbs, *Lectures on Study of Med. and Mod. Hist.*, 335–81, reprinted in *Anglo-Am. Legal Hist.*, I., ch. viii.; P. and M., *Hist. of Eng. Law*, I., ch. v.; Maitland, *Canon Law in Eng.*; Morey, *Outlines of Roman Law*, 203–7.

On Roman Law in England:

P. and M., *Hist. of Eng. Law*, I., ch. v.; Holdsworth, *Hist. of Eng. Law*, II., 108–17; Scrutton, T. E., *Influence of Roman Law on the Law of England*, chaps. vi., x.–xiv., and Conclusion, reprinted in *Anglo-Am. Legal Hist.*, I., ch. vii.; Maitland, F. W., *Eng. Law and the Renaissance* (Rede Lecture, 1901), reprinted in *Anglo-Am. Legal Hist.*, I., ch. vi.; Bracton, edited by Sir Travers Twiss, Introduction; Guterbock, Carl, *Bracton and his Relation to the Roman Law*, trans. by Brinton Cox, Phila., 1866; Bryce, *Studies in Hist. and Juris.*, 860–86.

On Trial by Jury and its Development:

P. and M., *Hist. of Eng. Law*, I., 138–53; Thayer, *Prelim. Treatise on Evidence*, chaps. ii., iii., iv.; Holdsworth, *Hist. of Eng. Law*, I., 145–69; Forsythe, *Trial by Jury*; Stephen, *Hist. of Crim. Law of Eng.*, I., chaps. viii. and xv., *passim*; Carter, *Hist. of Eng. Legal Insti.*, ch. xxii. (Criminal Jury); and ch. xxiii. (Civil Jury); Taswell-Langmead, *Eng. Consti. Hist.*, 133–43; Medley, *Eng. Consti. Hist.*, 321–26.

On Legal Forms of Trial in the Twelfth Century:

The Oath or Compurgation or Wager of Law:

P. and M., *Hist. of Eng. Law*, II., 600–1, 634–6; Bigelow, *Hist. of Procedure in Eng.*, 301–8; Thayer, *Prelim. Treatise on Evidence*, ch. i., 24–34, reprinted in *Anglo-Am. Legal Hist.*, II., ch. xxxi.; Holdsworth, *Hist. of Eng. Law*, I., 136–40; Lea, H. C., *Superstition and Force*, ch. i.

The Ordeal:

P. and M., *Hist. of Eng. Law*, II., 598–9; Bigelow, *Hist. of Procedure in Eng.*, 322–6; Thayer, *Prelim. Treatise on Evidence*, ch. i., 34–9, reprinted in *Anglo-Am. Legal Hist.*, II., ch. xxxi.; Holdsworth, *Hist. of Eng. Law*, I., 142–3; Lea, H. C., *Superstition and Force*, ch. iii.; Stephen, *Hist. of Crim. Law of Eng.*, I., ch. iii.; Hall, *Court Life under the Plantagenets*, extract from ch. vi., reprinted in *Anglo-Am. Legal Hist.*, II., ch. xxxiii., 425–30.

The Battle or Duel:

P. and M., *Hist. of Eng. Law*, II., 600, 632–4; Thayer, *Prelim. Treatise on Evidence*, ch. i., 39–46; reprinted in *Anglo-Am. Legal Hist.*, II., ch. xxxi.; Blackstone, *Com.*, III., 338–41, and IV., 341–2; Bigelow, *Hist. of Procedure in Eng.*, 326–30;

Holdsworth, *Hist. of Eng. Law*, I., 140–2; Lea, H. C., *Superstition and Force*, ch. ii.; Stephen, *Hist. of Crim. Law*, I., ch. iii.; Neilson, *Trial by Combat.*

On Sanctuary:

Blackstone, *Com.*, IV., 332–3; P. and M., *Hist. of Eng. Law*, II., 590; Stephen, *Hist. of Crim. Law of Eng.*, I, 491–2.

On Benefit of Clergy:

P. and M., *Hist. of Eng. Law*, I., 441–57; Blackstone, *Com.*, IV., 365–74; Stephen, *Hist. of Crim. Law of Eng.*, I., 459–72.

CHAPTER III

GROWTH OF LAW FROM HENRY II. TO EDWARD I., 1154-1272

Growth of Law. During the period which divides the coronation of Henry II. (1154) from the coronation of Edward I. (1272) definite legislation was still an uncommon thing. Great as were the changes due to Henry's watchful and restless activity, they were changes that were effected without the pomp of solemn law-making. A few written or even spoken words communicated to his justices, those justices whom he was constantly sending to perambulate the country, might do great things, might institute new methods of procedure, might bring new classes of men and of things within the cognizance of the royal court. Some of his ordinances—or "assizes," as they were called—have come down to us; others we have lost. No one was at any great pains to preserve their text, because they were regarded, not as new laws, but as mere temporary instructions which might be easily altered. They soon sink into the mass of unenacted "common law." Even in the next, the thirteenth, century some of Henry's rules were regarded as traditional rules which had come down from a remote time, and which might be ascribed to the Conqueror, the Confessor, or any other king around whom a mist of fable had gathered.

Magna Carta. Thus it came about that the lawyers of Edward I.'s day—and that was the day in which a professional class of temporal lawyers first became prominent in England—thought of Magna Carta as the oldest statute of the realm, the first chapter in the written law of the land, the earliest of those texts the very words of which are law. And what they did their successors do at the present day.

The Great Charter stands in the forefront of our statute-book, though of late years a great deal of it has been repealed. And certainly it is worthy of its place. It is worthy of its place just because it is no philosophical or oratorical declaration of the rights of man, nor even of the rights of Englishmen, but an intensely practical document, the fit prologue for those intensely practical statutes which English Parliaments will publish in age after age.

What is more, it is a grand compromise, and a fit prologue for all those thousands of compromises in which the practical wisdom of the English race will always be expressing itself. Its very form is a compromise—in part that of a free grant of liberties made by the king, in part that of a treaty between him and his subjects, which is to be enforced against him if he breaks it. And then in its detailed clauses it must do something for all those sorts and conditions of men who have united to resist John's tyranny—for the bishop, the clerk, the baron, the knight, the burgess, the merchant—and there must be some give and take between these classes, for not all their interests are harmonious. But even in the Great Charter there is not much new law; indeed, its own theory of itself (if we may use such a phrase) is that the old law, which a lawless king has set at naught, is to be restored, defined, covenanted, and written.

Statutes of Merton and Marlbridge. The Magna Carta of our statute-book[1] is not exactly the charter that John sealed at Runnymede; it is a charter granted by his son and successor, Henry III., the text of the original document having been modified on more than one occasion. Only two other acts of Henry's long reign attained the rank of statute law. The Provisions of Merton (1236), enacted by a great assembly of prelates and nobles, introduced several novelties, and contain those famous words, "We will

[1] "It is in the form in which it was promulgated in the 9th Henry III. that Magna Charta was confirmed by Edward I., in the twenty-fifth year of his reign. The copy which heads our statute-book is taken from an *inspeximus* of the Charter, so called from the letters patent prefixed in the name of Edward I."—Taswell-Langmead, *Eng. Consti. Hist.*, 119.

not have the laws of England changed," which were the reply of the barons to a request made by the bishops, who were desirous that our insular rule, "Once a bastard always a bastard," might yield to the law of the universal Church, and that marriage might have a retroactive effect. Among Englishmen there was no wish to change the laws of England. If only the king and his foreign favourites would observe those laws, then—such was the common opinion—all would be well.

A change came; vague discontent crystallized in the form of definite grievances. After the Barons' War the king, though he had triumphed over his foes, and was enjoying his own again, was compelled to redress many of those grievances by the Provisions of Marlborough (1267) or, as they have been commonly called, the Statute of Marlbridge.

When, a few years afterwards, Henry died (1272), the written, the enacted law of England consisted in the main of but four documents, which we can easily read through in half an hour—there was the Great Charter, there was the sister-charter which defined the forest law,[1] there were the Statutes of Merton and of "Marlbridge." To these we might

[1] "No Forest Charter was issued by John separately from the Forest clauses (44, 47, 48) of the Magna Charta. . . . The first Forest Charter was issued by the Earl of Pembroke, in Hen. III.'s name on 16th of Nov., 1217."—Taswell-Langmead, *Consti. Hist. of Eng.*, n. 117.

add a few minor ordinances; but the old Anglo-
Saxon dooms were by this time utterly forgotten,
the law-books of the Norman age were already unintelligible, and even the assizes of Henry II.,
though but a century old, had become part and
parcel of the "common law," not to be distinguished
from the unenacted rules which had gathered round
them. Englishmen might protest that they would
not change the law of England, but as a matter of
fact the law of England was being changed very
rapidly by the incessant decisions of the powerful
central court.

[**Triumph of Royal Justice.** "The king's courts
have been fast becoming the only judicial tribunals
of any great importance. Throughout the reign the
bulk of their plea rolls increased at a rapid rate.
Every term the bench at Westminster entertained a
multitude of causes. The litigants who came before
it were often men of lowly rank who were quarrelling
about small parcels of land. Though we hear some
bad stories of corrupt and partial judges, it is plain
that this powerful, central tribunal must have been
well trusted by the nation at large. Rich and poor
alike would go to it if they could. The local courts
were being starved, and this result we cannot ascribe
altogether to the ambition or greed of the lawyers at
Westminster. Of his own free will the small free-
holder passed by his lord's court and the county

6

court on his way to the great hall. He could here
obtain a stronger and better commodity than any
that was to be had elsewhere, a justice which, as
men reckoned in those days, was swift and masterful;
he could there force his adversary to submit to a
verdict instead of finding that his claim was met by
some antique oath with oath-helpers. The voice of
the nation, or what made itself heard as such, no
longer, as in 1215, demanded protection for the
seignorial courts; it asked that the royal court should
be endowed with yet new and anti-feudal powers;
it was to be in all temporal causes supreme. Men
were fast coming to the opinion that it ought to be,
in Bentham's phrase, 'omnicompetent,' and that
for every wrong there should be a remedy in the
court of their lord the king. This is not an idea that
is imposed from above upon an unwilling people.
Bracton himself, the royal judge, the professional
lawyer, does not thrust it forward as an obvious
principle. He explains or even apologizes for certain
manifestations of kingly justice which may seem to
be at variance with feudal rules. But still this
principle is at work: it is the king's business to
provide a competent remedy for every wrong."]—
P. and M., *Hist. of Eng. Law*, I., 202–3.

[**The Growth of the Common Law.** The process
by which during this period various district customs
gradually gave way to general custom and how such

custom when recognized by the powerful central court became the common law of England is thus described by Sir Frederick Pollock[1]:

"As time went on the popular courts faded into insignificance, then into oblivion; the name and functions of the ancient doomsmen vanished, and the law was delivered in the king's courts by the king's justices. We have already said that an impartial observer in the thirteenth century might well have expected the jury to become a strictly official piece of machinery. Not less might he have expected the king's judges to regard themselves and to be regarded as mere exponents of the king's will, and to prefer the interests of the Crown to all other considerations. But it fell out quite otherwise. Professional tradition and public spirit were too strong·for royal influence. As early as the thirteenth century the judges were the servants of the law first and the king afterwards. . . .

"Certainly the power of the king's judges, a compact body of learned persons directly representing the king's authority, was very great. Their office was, and is, deliberately exalted. To this day justices of assize take precedence, while they are on their circuit, of all other persons in the county. No less certainly the judicial power was used with great freedom to repress diversity of local customs and

[1] *Expansion of the Common Law*, 46–50.

establish uniform rules as far as the jurisdiction of the king's courts extended. But the courts were really doing the work of the ancient tradition, inasmuch as the uniformity which they established was not according to the king's pleasure, but according to law, and was far more capable of resisting executive interference than the customs which it superseded. If rival provincial customs had been allowed to take defined form, they might have invited an overruling despot. The Custom of the Realm was another matter. . . .

" A further development, already foreseen in the thirteenth century and settled beyond questioning in the fifteenth, is that which gives our jurisprudence its most peculiar and striking character. Judicial interpretation of the law is the only authentic interpretation. So far as the particular case is concerned this may seem an obvious matter. Positively, the court is there for the purpose of deciding, and has to arrive at a decision. Negatively, no other authority has any right to interfere with a court of justice acting within its competence; this is perhaps not quite so obvious, but may be supposed to be the rule in all or very nearly all civilized jurisdictions. But the Common Law goes much beyond this immediate respect for judicial authority. The judgment looks forward as well as backward. It not only ends the strife of the parties but lays down the law for similar

cases in the future. The opinion of a Superior Court
embodied in the reasons of its judgment stands, with
us, on a wholly different footing from any other form
of learned opinion. I am not aware that any historical reason can be given for this other than the
early consolidation of royal jurisdiction in England,
and the administration of justice by the king's
judges on a uniform system throughout the country.
Probably we shall never know how much they simplified, or whether their methods were always what we
should now call strictly judicial. But we know that
in the time of Henry I. it was still possible to talk of
district bodies of custom as existing in Wessex, in
Mercia, and in the Danelaw; that in the time of
Henry II. there were still undefined varieties of
usage, which may or may not have been confined to
procedure and to the rules of inheritance; and that
in the time of Henry III. men spoke only of the laws
and customs of England, and whatever did not
conform to the Common Law as declared by the
king's court had to justify itself as an exception on
some special ground. The king's judges, and they
alone, had power to lay down what the general
custom of England, in other words the Common Law,
for the terms are synonymous in our books, must be
taken to be. Quite possibly their own views of
convenience counted for something in the process of
determination; at the same time it is certain that, so

far as universal or very general usage really existed, the king's judges, doing the king's business in all parts of the country and comparing their experience at Westminster, were the persons best qualified to know it. The law of the thirteenth century was judge-made law in a fuller and more literal sense than the law of any succeeding century has been. Laymen sometimes talk of judge-made law as if judges were legislators and could lay down any rule they chose. It is needless to explain to a legal audience that this is not so. Judges are indeed bound to find some rule for deciding every case that comes before them, but they must do it without contradicting established principles, and in conformity with the reasons on which previous decisions were founded. They may supplement and enlarge the law as they find it, or rather they must do so from time to time, as the novelty of questions coming before them may require; but they must not reverse what has been settled. Only express legislation can do that. But even now there are a certain number of cases "of the first impression." In the thirteenth century their number was large.

"Henry III.'s and Edward I.'s judges did not rejoice in, or groan under, a library of printed reports; they had many new cases and little recorded authority, and were almost compelled to be original. But they certainly intended to be consistent, and were aware that their judgments were regarded as fixing the law. One reason why judicial precedents acquired exclusive authority was the absence of any other source of law capable of competing with them. Legislation was still exceptional and occasional, and there was no independent learned class. When the king's court began to keep its rolls in due course, the rolls themselves were the only evidence of the principles by which the court was guided; and the earliest treatises on the Common Law were produced by members of the judicial staff, or under their direction. It is also to be considered that the king's courts, as their functions became defined, had to regulate their own procedure if there was to be any order at all in their business; and that, in a state of government where both law and procedure are new, it is hard to draw an exact line between them, or to provide for urgent matters of procedure without determining the bent of the law itself. . . .

" Thus the king's courts were driven, in more than one way, to be self-sufficient. Willing or not, they would still have had to make their own practice, and in doing so they could not help making a good deal of law."]

READINGS

On Assizes of Henry II.:
  P. and M., *Hist. of Eng. Law*, I., 137–8, 145–50; Stubbs, *Consti. Hist. of Eng.*, I., Index; Carter, *Hist. Eng. Legal Insti.*, ch. viii.; Thayer, *Evidence at Common Law*, Index, "Assizes"; Holdsworth, *Hist. of Eng. Law*, I., 21, and II., 138–44.

  For text of assizes of Clarendon, Northampton, Arms and Forest, see Stubbs, *Select Charters*, 140–59.

On Events Leading to Magna Charta, with Analysis of its Provisions:
  McKechnie, W. S., *Magna Carta*, 1–57; Stubbs, *Consti. Hist. of Eng.*, I., 513–44; Taswell-Langmead, *Eng. Consti. Hist.*, ch. iv.

  For text of Magna Charta, see *Statutes of the Realm*, I.; Stubbs, *Select Charters*, 296–306; McKechnie, W. S., *Magna Carta* (Text, Translation, and Commentary), 215–564; Taswell-Langmead, *Eng. Consti. Hist.*, ch. iv. (Analysis, Summary, and Commentary).

  For Texts of Statutes of Merton and of Marlbridge, see *Statutes of the Realm*, I. For summary of their provisions see Holdsworth, *Hist. of Eng. Law*, II., 173–4.

On Magna Charta and the History of English Law as a Branch of Politics:
  Pollock, *Essays in Jurisprudence and Ethics*, ch. viii.

On Growth of the King's Courts from Beginning of Reign of Henry II. (1154) to end of that of Edward I. (1307):
  P. and M., *Hist. of Eng. Law*, I., 153–60, 190–203; Carter, *Hist. of Eng. Legal Insti.*, ch. ix.; Taswell-Langmead, *Eng. Consti. Hist.*, 129–32.

On Legal Effects of the Norman Conquest and Process by which the
   Custom of the King's Court became the Common Law
   of England:
   Appendix II.; also P. and M., *Hist. of Eng. Law*, I., 107–10
   and 174–203; Holdsworth, *Hist. of Eng. Law*, II., 107–69; Pol-
   lock, *First Book of Juris.*, 240–3; Jenks, *Edward I.*, 339–46;
   Medley, *Eng. Consti. Hist.*, ch. vii., 318–39; Taswell-Langmead,
   Eng. Consti. Hist., chaps. ii. and v. *passim.*

CHAPTER IV

LEGAL REFORM UNDER EDWARD I. AND THE SYSTEM OF WRITS, 1272–1307

Legal Reform under Edward I. and the System of Writs. On Henry's death there followed some eighteen years which even at this day may seem to us the most brilliant eighteen years in the whole history of English legislation. At all events, if we are to find a comparable period we must look forward, for five hundred years and more, to the age of the first Reform Bill. Year by year King Edward I. in his Parliaments made laws on a grand scale. His statutes will not be in our eyes very lengthy documents; but they are drastic, and they are permanent. They deal with all sorts of matters, public and private, but in particular with those elementary parts of the law of property and the law of civil procedure which English legislators have, as a general rule, been well content to leave alone. Just for this reason they are exceedingly permanent; they become fundamental; elaborate edifices of gloss and comment are reared upon them. To this day, despite all the reforms of

the last century, we have to look to them, and the
interpretation which has been set upon them, for
some of the most elementary principles of our land
law.   When all has been said that can be said for the
explanation of this unique outburst of legislation, it
still remains a marvellous thing.

[**The Legislation of Edward I.**   This legislation is
thus described by Prof. T. F. Tout in his *Edward the
First*, 122–3:

"Since Henry II. had first systematized and
arranged the legal system which grew out of the
Norman Conquest, there had been a century of rapid
development, fruitful in great and original ideas, but
throwing out its results without order or method,
and with little care for clearness or consistency.
English law had grown like a great wood where the
trees stand so close together that none attain their
proper proportions, and where a rich tangle of under-
wood blocks up all paths and access.   It was the
work of Edward and his ministers to prune away this
too luxuriant growth.   Their work was a task of
ordering, of methodizing, of arranging.   Edward's
age was, as Bishop Stubbs tells us, a period of definition.   His aim was to group together and codify, in
such informal ways as the spirit of his age and
country allowed, the legal system which had grown
up in disorderly abundance in the previous genera-
tions.   His well-known title of the 'English Jus-

tinian' is not so absurd as it appears at first sight. He did not merely resemble Justinian in being a great legislator. Like the famous codifier of the Roman law, Edward stood at the end of a long period of legal development, and sought to arrange and systematize what had gone before him. Some of his great laws are almost in form attempts at the systematic codification of various branches of feudal custom. The whole of his legislation is permeated by a spirit which is at bottom essentially the same as the impulse which makes for codification. We shall therefore seek in vain for anything very new or revolutionary in Edward's legislation. We shall find a minute adaptation of means to ends, a spirit of definition and classification rather than any great originality or insight. But Edward did just what was most wanted at the time, and his work became all the more important and lasting because of its narrow adaptation to the needs and circumstances of his age."]

Growth of a Legal Profession. A professional class of English temporal lawyers was just beginning to form itself. We say "of English temporal lawyers," because for more than a century past there had been "legists" and "decretists" in the land.

These legists and decretists constituted a professional class; they held themselves out as willing to plead the causes of those who would pay their

fees. They did a large business, for the clergy of the
time were extremely litigious. The bishop who was
not perennially engaged in interminable disputes
with two or three wealthy religious houses was either
a very fortunate or a very careless guardian of the
rights of his see. And all the roads of ecclesiastical
litigation led to Rome. Appeals to the Pope were
made at every stage of every cause, and the
most famous Italian lawyers were retained as
advocates.

The King of England, who was often involved in
contests about the election of bishops—contests
which would sooner or later come before the Roman
Curia—kept Italian canonists in his pay. Young
Englishmen were sent to Bologna in order that they
might learn the law of the Church. The University
of Oxford was granting degrees in civil and canon
law, the University of Cambridge followed her
example. There was no lack of ecclesiastical lawyers;
indeed, the wisest and most spiritual of the clergy
thought that there were but too many of them, and
deplored that theology was neglected in favour of a
more lucrative science. And what we might call an
ecclesiastical "Bar" had been formed. The canonist
who wished to practise in a bishop's court had to
satisfy the bishop of his competence, and to take an
oath obliging him to practise honestly. The tribunals
of the Church knew both the "advocate" (who pleads

on behalf of a client) and the "procurator" or "proctor" (who represents his client's person and attends to his cause).

Attorneys and Barristers. In course of time two groups similar to these grew up round the king's court. We see the "attorney" (who answers to the ecclesiastical proctor) and the "pleader," "narrator," or "countor" (who answers to the ecclesiastical advocate). But the formation of these classes of professional lawyers has not been easy. Ancient law does not readily admit that one man can represent another; in particular, it does not readily admit that one man can represent another in litigation. So long as procedure is extremely formal, so long as all depends on the due utterance of sacramental words, it does not seem fair that you should put an expert in your place to say those words for you. My adversary has, as it were, a legal interest in my ignorance or stupidity. If I cannot bring my charge against him in due form, that charge ought to fail; at all events, he cannot justly be called upon to answer another person, some subtle and circumspect pleader, whom I have hired. Thus the right to appoint an attorney who will represent my person in court, and win or lose my cause for me, appears late in the day. It spreads outwards from the king. From of old the king must be represented by others in his numerous suits. This right of his he can confer upon his subjects—at first as an exceptional favour, and afterwards by a general rule.

In Henry III.'s reign this process has gone thus far: a litigant in the king's court may appoint an attorney to represent him in the particular action in which he is for the time being engaged; he requires no special licence for this; but if a man wishes to prospectively appoint a general attorney, who will represent him in all actions, the right to do this he must buy from the king, and he will not get it except for some good cause. The attorneys of this age are by no means always professional men of business. Probably every free and lawful man may act as the attorney of another; indeed, shocking as this may seem to us, we may, not very unfrequently, find a wife appearing in court as her husband's attorney.

The other "branch of the profession" grows from a different stock. In very old days a litigant is allowed to bring his friends into court, and to take "counsel" with them before he speaks. Early in the twelfth century it is already the peculiar mark of a capital accusation, that the accused must answer without "counsel." Then sometimes one of my friends will be allowed, not merely to prompt me, but even to speak for me.

It is already seen that the old requirement of extreme verbal accuracy is working injustice. A man ought to have some opportunity of amending a

mere slip of the tongue; and yet old legal principles
will not suffer that he should amend the slips of his
own tongue. Let another tongue slip for him. Such
is the odd compromise between ancient law and
modern equity. One great advantage that I gain
by putting forward "one of my counsel" to speak for
me is that if he blunders—if, for example, he speaks
of Roger when he should have spoken of Richard—
I shall be able to correct the mistake, for his words
will not bind me until I have adopted them. Naturally, however, I choose for this purpose my acutest
and most experienced friends. Naturally, also, acute
and experienced men are to be found who will gladly
be for this purpose my friends or anybody else's
friends, if they be paid for their friendliness. As a
class of expert pleaders forms itself, the relation
between the litigant and those who "are of counsel for
him" will be very much changed, but it will not lose
all traces of its friendly character. Theoretically one
cannot hire another person to plead for one; in other
words, counsel cannot sue for his fees.

Serjeants-at-Law. Seemingly, it was in the reign
of Henry III. that pleaders seeking for employment
began to cluster round the king's court. Some of
them the king, the busiest of all litigants, kept in his
pay; they were his "serjeants"—that is, servants—
at law.

Under Edward I. a process, the details of which

are still very obscure, was initiated by the king, which brought these professional pleaders and the professional attorneys under the control of the judges, and began to secure a monopoly of practice to those who had been formally ordained to the ministry of the law. About the same time it is that we begin to read of men climbing from the Bar to the Bench, and about the same time it is that the judges are ceasing to be ecclesiastics.

If we look back to Richard I.'s reign we may see, as the highest temporal court of the realm, a court chiefly composed of ecclesiastics, presided over by an archbishop, who is also Chief Justiciar; he will have at his side two or three bishops, two or three arch-deacons, and but two or three laymen. The greatest judges even of Henry III.'s reign are ecclesiastics, though by this time it has become scandalous for a bishop to do much secular justice. These judges have deserved their appointments, not by pleading for litigants, but by serving as clerks in the court, the Exchequer, the Chancery. They are professionally learned in the law of the land, but they have acquired their skill rather as the civil servants of the Crown than as the advocates or advisers of private persons; and if they serve the king well on the Bench, they may hope to retire upon bishoprics, or at all events deaneries.

But the Church has been trying to withdraw the

clergy from this work in the civil courts. Very curious had been the shifts to which ecclesiastics had been put in order to keep themselves technically free of blood-guiltiness. The accused criminal knew what was going to happen when the ecclesiastical president of the court rose, but left his lay associates behind him. Hands that dared not write "and the jurors say that he is guilty, and therefore let him be hanged," would go so far as "and therefore, etc." Lips that dared not say any worse would venture a sufficiently intelligible "Take him away, and let him have a priest." However, the Church has her way. The clerks of the court, the Exchequer, the Chancery, will for a very long time be clerks in holy orders; but before the end of Edward I.'s reign the appointment of an ecclesiastic to be one of the king's justices will be becoming rare.

On the whole, we may say that from that time to the present, one remarkable characteristic of our legal system is fixed—all the most important work of the law is done by a very small number of royal justices who have been selected from the body of pleaders practising in the king's courts.

The King's Courts. Slowly the "curia" of the Norman reigns had been giving birth to various distinct offices and tribunals. In Edward's day there was a "King's Bench" (a court for criminal causes and other "pleas of the Crown"); a "Common

Bench" (a court for actions brought by one subject against another); an Exchequer, which both in a judicial and an administrative way collected the king's revenue and enforced his fiscal rights; a Chancery, which was a universal secretarial bureau, doing all the writing that was done in the king's name.   These various departments had many adventures to live through before the day would come when they would once more be absorbed into a High Court of Justice.   Of some few of those adventures we shall speak in another place, but must here say two or three words about a matter which gave a distinctive shape to the whole body of our law—a shape that it is even now but slowly losing.

System of Writs.   Our common law during the later Middle Ages and far on into modern times is in the main a commentary on writs issued out of the King's Chancery.[1]   To understand this, we must go back to the twelfth century, to a time when it would have seemed by no means natural that ordinary litigation between ordinary men should come into the king's court.   It does not come there without an order from the king.   Your adversary could not summon you to meet him in that court; the summons must come from the king.

---

[1] "The first extant Register of Writs dates from 1227, but, doubtless, earlier registers have existed for some time in the archives of the Court."—Jenks, *Law and Politics in Middle Ages*, 38.

Thus much of the old procedure we still retain in our own time; it will be the reigning King, not your creditor, who will bid you appear in his High Court. But whereas at the present day the formal part of the writ will merely bid you appear in court, and all the information that you will get about the nature of the claim against you will be conveyed to you in the plaintiff's own words or those of his legal advisers, this was not so until very lately. In old times the writ that was drawn up in the King's Chancery and sealed with his great seal told the defendant a good many particulars about the plaintiff's demand. Gradually, as the king began to open the doors of his court to litigants of all kinds, blank forms of the various writs that could be issued were accumulated in the Chancery. We may think of the king as keeping a shop in which writs were sold. Some of them were to be had at fixed prices, or, as we should say nowadays, they could be had as matters of course on the payment of fixed court-fees; for others special bargains had to be made. Then, in course of time, as our Parliamentary constitution took shape, the invention of new writs became rarer and rarer. Men began to see that if the king in his Chancery could devise new remedies by granting new writs, he had in effect a power of creating new rights and making new laws without the concurrence of the estates of the realm. And so it came to be a settled doctrine that though the old formulas might be modified in immaterial particulars to suit new cases as they arose, no new formula could be introduced except by statute.

This change had already taken place in Edward I.'s day. Thenceforward the cycle of writs must be regarded as a closed cycle; no one can bring his cause before the king's courts unless he can bring it within the scope of one of those formulas which the Chancery has in stock and ready for sale. We may argue that if there is no writ there is no remedy, and if there is no remedy there is no wrong; and thus the register of writs in the Chancery becomes the test of rights and the measure of law. Then round each writ a great mass of learning collects itself. He who knows what cases can be brought within each formula knows the law of England. The body of law has a skeleton and that skeleton is the system of writs. Thus our jurisprudence took an exceedingly rigid and permanent shape; it became a commentary on formulas. It could still grow and assimilate new matter, but it could only do this by a process of interpretation which gradually found new, and not very natural, meanings for old phrases. As we shall see hereafter, this process of interpretation was too slow to keep up with the course of social and economic change, and the Chancery had to come to the relief of the courts of law by making itself a court of equity.

READINGS

On Edward I., the English Justinian, and the Definition of the
  Sphere of the Common Law:
  Digby, *Hist. of Real Property*, ch. iv.; Stubbs, *Consti. Hist. of
  Eng.*, II., 100–19; Jenks, *Edward Plantagenet*, chaps. ix. and
  xiii., reprinted in *Anglo-Am. Legal Hist.*, I., ch. v.; Holdsworth,
  Hist. of Eng. Law, II., 236–61 *passim*, and 290–312; Carter,
  Hist. of Eng. Legal Insti., ch. x.; Tout, *Edward I.*, ch. vii.

On the Original Writ, and the Requirement of a New Statute to
  Introduce New Formulas:
  P. and M., *Hist. of Eng. Law*, I., 150–1 and 195–7; II., 564–8;
  Medley, *Eng. Consti. Hist.*, 319–21; Carter, *Hist. of Eng. Legal
  Insti.* (1st ed., 1902), Appendix I., The Writ in Consimili Casu;
  Jenks, *Law and Politics in Mid. Ages*, 122–25.

CHAPTER V

GROWTH OF STATUTE AND COMMON LAW AND RISE
OF THE COURT OF CHANCERY, 1307–1600

The Idea of Law in the Middle Ages. The desire
for continuous legislation is modern. We have
come to think that, year by year, Parliament must
meet and pour out statutes; that every statesman
must have in his mind some programme of new
laws; that if his programme once became exhausted
he would cease to be a statesman. It was otherwise
in the Middle Ages. As a matter of fact a parliament might always find that some new statute was
necessary. The need for legislation, however, was
occasioned (so men thought) not by any fated progress of the human race, but by the perversity of
mankind. Ideally there exists a perfect body of law,
immutable, eternal, the work of God, not of man.
Just a few more improvements in our legal procedure
will have made it for ever harmonious with this ideal;
and, indeed, if men would but obey the law of the
land as it stands, there would be little for a legislator
to do.

103

Legislation in the Fourteenth Century. During the fourteenth century a good deal is written upon the statute roll, and a good deal can still be said in very few words. "Also it is agreed that a parliament shall be holden once a year or more often if need be."[1] This is a characteristic specimen of the brief sentences in which great principles are formulated and which by their ambiguity will provide the lawyers and politicians of later ages with plenty of matter for debate. Many of these short clauses are directed against what are regarded as abuses, as evasions of the law, and the king's officers are looked upon as the principal offenders. They must be repeated with but little variation from time to time, for it is difficult to bind the king by law. Happily the kings were needy; in return for "supply" they sold the words on the statute roll, and those words, of some importance when first conceded, became of far greater importance in after times. When we read them nowadays they turn our thoughts to James and Charles, rather than to Edward and Richard. The "New Monarchy"

[1] "As the political functions of the national parliament became more prominently important than the judicial work of the king in his full council, it became a point of public security that regular and fairly frequent parliaments should be held; and the demand for annual parliaments accordingly emerges very soon after the final admission of representatives of the commons. . . . The ordinances of 1311 and the acts of Parliament in 1330 and 1362 established the rule that parliaments should be held annually and oftener if it were found necessary."—Stubbs, *Consti. Hist. of Eng.*, III., 380, par. 733.

was not new. This, from its own point of view, was its great misfortune. It had inherited ancient parchment rolls which had uncomfortable words upon them.

Its Scope. But Parliament by its statutes was beginning to interfere with many affairs, small as well as great. Indeed, what we may consider small affairs seem to have troubled and interested it more even than those large constitutional questions which it was always hoping to settle but never settling. If we see a long statute, one guarded with careful provisos, one that tells us of debate and compromise, this will probably be a statute which deals with one particular trade; for example, a statute concerning the sale of herring at Yarmouth fair. The thorniest of themes for discussion is the treatment of foreign merchants. Naturally enough our lords, knights, and burgesses cannot easily agree about it. One opinion prevails in the seaports, another in the up- land towns, and the tortuous course of legislation, swaying now towards Free Trade and now towards Protection, is the resultant of many forces. The "omnicompetence," as Bentham called it, of statute law was recognized by all, the impotence of statute law was seen by none. It can determine the rate of wages, the price of goods, the value of money; it can decide that no man shall dress himself above his station.

On the other hand, the great outlines of criminal law and private law seem to have been regarded as fixed for all time. In the present century students of law will still for practical purposes be compelled to know a good deal about some of the statutes of Edward I. They will seldom have occasion to know anything of any laws that were enacted during the fourteenth or the first three-quarters of the fifteenth century. Parliament seems to have abandoned the idea of controlling the development of the common law. Occasionally and spasmodically it would interfere, devise some new remedy, fill a gap in the register of writs, or circumvent the circumventors of a statute. But in general it left the ordinary law of the land to the judges and the lawyers. In its eyes the common law was complete, or very nearly complete.

And then as we read the statute-roll of the fifteenth century we seem for a while to be watching the decline and fall of a mighty institution. Parliament seems to have nothing better to do than to regulate the manufacture of cloth. Now and then it strives to cope with the growing evils of the time, the renascent feudalism, the private wars of great and small; but without looking outside our roll we can see that these efforts are half-hearted and ineffectual. We are expected to show a profound interest in "the making of worsteds," while we gather from a few casual hints that the Wars of the Roses are flagrant.

If for a moment the Parliament of Edward IV. can raise its soul above defective barrels of fish and fraudulent gutter tiles this will be in order to prohibit "cloish, kayles, half-bowl, hand-in-hand and hand-out, quekeboard," and such other games as interfere with the practice of archery.

The Omnipotence of Parliament. In the end it was better that Parliament should for a while register the acts of a despot than that it should sink into the contempt that seemed to be prepared for it. The part which the assembled estates of the realm have to play in the great acts of Henry VIII. (1509–47) may in truth be a subservient and ignoble part; but the acts are great and they are all done "by the authority of Parliament." By the authority of Parliament the Bishop of Rome could be deprived of all jurisdiction, the monasteries could be dissolved, the king could be made (so far as the law of God would permit) supreme head of the English Church, the succession to the Crown could be settled first in this way, then in that, the force of statute might be given to the king's proclamations. There was nothing that could not be done by the authority of Parliament. And apart from the constitutional and ecclesiastical changes which everyone has heard about, very many things of importance were done by statute.

We owe to Henry VIII.—much rather to him than to his Parliament—not a few innovations in the law of property and the law of crime, and the parliaments of Elizabeth performed some considerable legal exploits. The statutes of the Tudor period are lengthy documents. In many a grandiose preamble we seem to hear the voice of Henry himself; but their length is not solely due to the pomp of imperial phrases. They condescend to details; they teem with exceptions and saving clauses. One cannot establish a new ecclesiastical polity by half-a-dozen lines. We see that the judges are by this time expected to attend very closely to the words that Parliament utters, to weigh and obey every letter of the written law.

Statute and Common Law. Just now and then in the last of the Middle Ages and thence onwards into the eighteenth century, we hear the judges claiming some vague right of disregarding statutes which are directly at variance with the common law, or the law of God, or the royal prerogative. Had much come of this claim, our constitution must have taken a very different shape from that which we see at the present day. Little came of it. In the troublous days of Richard II. a chief justice got himself hanged as a traitor for advising the king that a statute curtailing the royal power was void. For the rest, the theory is but a speculative dogma. We can (its upholders seem to say) conceive that a statute might be so irrational, so wicked, that we would not enforce it; but, as a matter of fact, we have never known such a statute made. From the Norman Conquest onwards, England seems marked out as the country in which men, so soon as they begin to philosophize, will endeavour to prove that all law is the command of a "sovereign one," or a "sovereign many." They may be somewhat shocked when in the seventeenth century Hobbes states this theory in trenchant terms and combines it with many unpopular doctrines.[1] But the way for Hobbes had been prepared of old. In the days of Edward I. the text-writer, whom we call Britton, had put the common law into the king's mouth: all legal rules might be stated as royal commands.

Still, even in the age of the Tudors, only a small part of the law was in the statute-book. Detached pieces of superstructure were there; for the foundation men had to look elsewhere. After the brilliant thirteenth century a long, dull period had set in. The custody of the common law was now committed to a small group of judges and lawyers. They knew their own business very thoroughly, and they knew nothing else. Law was now divorced from literature; no one attempted to write a book about it. The decisions of the courts at Westminster were diligently reported and

[1] For description of political philosophy of Hobbes, and theory of sovereignty in England, see Pollock, *Hist. of Science of Politics*, 55-65; *First Book of Juris.*, ch. iii.; and Bryce, *Studies in Hist. and Juris.*, Essay x. *passim*.

diligently studied, but no one thought of comparing English law with anything else.[1] Roman law was by this time an unintelligible, outlandish thing, perhaps a good enough law for half-starved Frenchmen.

The Legal Profession: The Inns of Court. Legal education was no longer academic—the universities had nothing to do with it, they could only make canonists and civilians—it was scholastic. By stages that are exceedingly obscure, the inns of court and inns of chancery were growing. They were associations of lawyers which had about them a good deal of the club, something of the college, something of the trade-union. They acquired the "inns" or "hospices"—that is, the town houses—which had belonged to great noblemen: for example, the Earl of Lincoln's inn. The house and church of the Knights of the Temple came to their hands. The smaller societies, "inns of chancery," became dependent on the larger societies, "inns of court."[2] The serjeants and apprentices who composed them enjoyed an

---

[1] "There is no proof that reports of the cases were taken down at the time, for ordinary professional use, before the late years of the thirteenth century. . . . From the year 1292 we have a series of reports of cases decided, partly by Edward I.'s judges on their circuits 'in eyre,' partly before the Courts at Westminster."— Pollock, *First Book of Juris.*, 278-9.

For description of these reports known as Year Books, which extend with some breaks from 1292 in the reign of Edward I., to 28, Hen. VIII., 1537, see Pollock, *First Book of Juris.*, 278-86; Wallace *The Reporters*, 73-111.

[2] "What is distinctive of Mediæval England is not Parliament, for

exclusive right of pleading in court; some things
might be done by an apprentice or barrister, others
required a serjeant; in the Court of Common Pleas
only a serjeant could be heard. It would take time
to investigate the origin of that power of granting
degrees which these societies wielded. To all seeming the historian must regard it as emanating from
the king, though in this case, as in many other cases,
the control of a royal prerogative slowly passed out
of the king's hand. But here our point must be,
that the inns developed a laborious system of legal
education. Many years a student had to spend in
hearing and giving lectures and in pleading fictitious
causes before he could be admitted to practice.

It is no wonder that under the fostering care of
these societies English jurisprudence became an
occult science and its professors "the most unlearned
kind of most learned men." They were rigorous
logicians, afraid of no conclusion that was implicit
in their premises. The sky might fall, the Wars of
the Roses might rage, but they would pursue the
even course of their argumentation. They were not
altogether unmindful of the social changes that were
going on around them. In the fifteenth century
there were great judges who performed what may

we may everywhere see assemblies of Estates, nor trial by jury, for
this was but slowly suppressed in France. But the Inns of Court and
the Year Books that were read therein, we shall hardly find their
like elsewhere."—Maitland, *Eng. Law and the Renaissance*, 27.

seem to us some daring feats in the accommodation of old law to new times. Out of unpromising elements they developed a comprehensive law of contract; they loosened the bonds of those family settlements by which land had been tied up; they converted the precarious villein tenure of the Middle Ages into the secure copyhold tenure of modern times.[1] But all this had to be done evasively and by means of circumventive fictions. Novel principles could not be admitted until they were disguised in some antique garb.

A new and a more literary period seems to be beginning in the latter half of the fifteenth century when Sir John Fortescue,[2] the Lancastrian chief justice, writing for the world at large, contrasts the constitutional kingship of England with the absolute monarchy of France, and Sir Thomas Littleton, a justice in the Court of Common Pleas, writing for students of English law, publishes, in 1480 or 1481, his lucid and classical book on the tenure of land.[3]

---

[1] See Blackstone, *Com.*, topics of Contracts, Family Settlements, Copyhold, and Villein tenure.

[2] See Campbell, *Lives of the Lord Chancellors of Eng.*, I., ch. xxii.; and Life of Fortescue, by Lord Clermont prefixed to *De Laudibus Legum Angliæ*, Cincinnati, 1874.

For Fortescue's theory of the English Constitution, see *De Laudibus Legum Angliæ*, cc. 9, 13, quoted in Taswell-Langmead, *Eng. Consti. Hist.*, 301-2.

[3] Sir Thomas Littleton was born in the early years of the fifteenth century, exact date unknown, and died August 23, 1481. For description of this famous book, see Wambaugh, *Intro. to Littleton's Tenures*, 11-63.

But the hopes of a renascence are hardly fulfilled. In the sixteenth century many famous lawyers added to their fame by publishing reports of decided cases and by making "abridgments" of the old reports, and a few little treatises were compiled; but in general the lawyer seems to think that he has done all for jurisprudence that can be done when he has collected his materials under a number of rubrics alphabetically arranged.[1]   The alphabet is the one clue to the maze.

Even in the days of Elizabeth and James I. Sir Edward Coke, the incarnate common law, shovels out his enormous learning in vast disorderly heaps. Carlyle's felicity has for ever stamped upon Coke the adjective "tough"—"tough old Coke upon Littleton, one of the toughest men ever made." We may well transfer the word from the man to the law that was personified in him.   The English common law was tough, one of the toughest things ever made. And well for England was it in the days of Tudors and Stuarts that this was so.   A simpler, a more rational, a more elegant system would have been an apt instrument of despotic rule.   At times the judges were subservient enough: the king could dismiss them from their offices at a moment's notice; but the clumsy, cumbrous system, though it might bend,

---

[1] For the probable contents of an English lawyer's library in 1550, see Maitland, *Eng. Law and the Renaissance*, 90, note 62.

8

would never break. It was ever awkwardly re-
bounding and confounding the statecraft which had
tried to control it. The strongest king, the ablest
minister, the rudest lord-protector could make little
of this "ungodly jumble."

Growth of the Judicial System. To this we must
add that professional jealousies had been aroused by
the evolution of new courts, which did not proceed
according to the course of the common law. Once
more we must carry our thoughts back to the days of
Edward I. The three courts—King's Bench, Common Bench, and Exchequer—had been established.
There were two groups of "Justices," and one group
of "Barons" engaged in administering the law.

House of Lords. But behind these courts there
was a tribunal of a less determinate nature. Looking
at it in the last years of the thirteenth century we
may doubt as to what it is going to be. Will it be a
house of magnates, an assembly of the lords spiritual
and temporal, or will it be a council composed of the
king's ministers and judges and those others whom
he pleases for one reason or another to call to the
council board? As a matter of fact, in Edward I.'s
day, this highest tribunal seems to be rather the
council than the assembly of prelates and barons.
This council is a large body; it comprises the great
officers of state—chancellor, treasurer, and so forth;
it comprises the judges of the three courts; it com-

prises also the masters or chief clerks of the chancery, whom he may liken to the "permanent under-secretaries" of our own time; it comprises also those prelates and barons whom the king thinks fit to have about him. But the definition of this body seems somewhat vague. The sessions or "parliaments" in which it does justice often coincide in time with those assemblies of the estates of the realm by which, in later days, the term "parliaments" is specifically appropriated, and at any moment it may take the form of a meeting to which not only the ordinary councillors, but all the prelates and barons, have been summoned.

In the light which later days throw back upon the thirteenth century we seem to see in the justiciary "parliaments" of Edward I. two principles, one of which we may call aristocratic, while the other is official; and we think that, sooner or later, there must be a conflict between them—that one must grow at the expense of the other. And then again we cannot see very plainly how the power of this tribunal will be defined, for it is doing work of a miscellaneous kind. Not only is it a court of last resort in which the errors of all lower courts can be corrected, but as a court of first instance it can entertain whatever causes, civil or criminal, the king may evoke before it. Then lastly, acting in a manner which to us seems half judicial and half administrative, it hears the numer-

ous petitions of those who will urge any claim against
the king, or complain of any wrong which cannot be
redressed in the formal course of ordinary justice.

In the course of the fourteenth century some of
these questions were settled. It became clear that
the Lords' House of Parliament, the assembly of
prelates and barons, was to be the tribunal which
could correct the mistakes in law committed by the
lower courts. The right of a peer of the realm to be
tried for capital crimes by a court composed of his
peers was established. Precedents were set for those
processes which we know as impeachments, in which
the House of Lords hears accusations brought by the
House of Commons. In all these matters, therefore,
a tribunal technically styled the "King in Parliament," but which was in reality the House of Lords
appeared as the highest tribunal of the realm. But,
beside it, we see another tribunal with indefinitely
wide claims to jurisdiction—we see the "King in
Council." And the two are not so distinct as an
historian, for his own sake and his readers', might
wish them to be.

Beginning of the Star Chamber. On the one hand,
those of the king's council who are not peers of the
realm, in particular the judges and the masters of
the chancery, are summoned to the Lords' House of
Parliament, and only by slow degrees is it made plain
to them that, when they are in that house, they are

mere "assistants" of the peers, and are only to speak when they are spoken to. On the other hand, there is a widespread, if not very practical, belief that all the peers are by rights the king's councillors, and that any one of them may sit at the council board if he pleases. Questions enough are left open for subsequent centuries.

Its Work and Use. Meanwhile the council, its actual constitution varying much from reign to reign, does a great deal of justice, for the more part criminal justice, and this it does in a summary, administrative way. Plainly there is great need for such justice, for though the representative commoners and the lawyers dislike it, they always stop short of demanding its utter abolition. The commoners protest against this or that abuse. Sometimes they seem to be upon the point of denouncing the whole institution as illegal; but then there comes some rebellion or some scandalous acquittal of a notorious criminal by bribed or partial jurors, which convinces them that, after all, there is a place for a masterful court which does not stand upon ceremony, which can strike rapidly and have no need to strike twice. They cannot be brought to openly admit that one main cause of the evils that they deplore is the capricious clumsiness of that trial by jury which has already become the theme of many a national boast. They will not legislate about the matter, rather they will look the other way while the council is punishing rich and powerful offenders, against whom no verdict could have been obtained. A hard line is drawn between the felonies, for which death is the punishment, and the minor offences. No one is to suffer loss of life or limb unless twelve of his neighbours have sworn to his guilt after a solemn trial; but the council must be suffered to deal out fines and imprisonments against rioters, conspirators, bribers, perjured jurors; otherwise there will be anarchy.

Its Procedure. The council evolves a procedure for such cases, or rather it uses the procedure of the canon law. It sends for the accused; it compels him to answer upon oath written interrogatories. Affidavits, as we should call them, are sworn upon both sides. With written depositions before them, the lords of the council, without any jury, acquit or convict. The extraction of confessions by torture is no unheard-of thing.

Its Iniquities. It was in a room known as the Star Chamber that the council sat when there was justice to be done, and there, as the "Court of Star Chamber," it earned its infamy. That infamy it fairly earned under the first two Stuart kings, and no one will dispute that the Long Parliament did well in abolishing it. It had become a political court and a cruel court, a court in which divines sought to impose their dogmas and their ritual upon a recalcitrant nation by heavy sentences; in which a king, endeavouring to rule without a Parliament, tried to give the force of statutes to his proclamations, to exact compulsory loans, to gather taxes that the Commons had denied him; a whipping, nose-slitting, ear-cropping court; a court with a grim, unseemly humour of its own, which would condemn to an exclusive diet of pork the miserable puritan who took too seriously the Mosaic prohibition of swine's flesh. And then, happily, there were doubts about its legality. The theory got about that it derived all its lawful powers from a statute passed in 1487, at the beginning of Henry VII.'s reign, while manifestly it was exceeding those powers in all directions. We cannot now accept that theory, unless we are prepared to say that for a century and a half all the great judges, including Coke himself, had taken an active part in what they knew to be the unlawful doings of the council—the two chief justices had habitually sat in the Star Chamber. Still we may be glad that this theory was accepted. The court was abolished in the name of the common law.

It had not added much to our national jurisprudence. It had held itself aloof from jurisprudence; it had been a law unto itself, with hands free to invent new remedies for every new disease of the body politic. It had little regard for precedents, and, therefore, men were not at pains to collect its decisions. It had, however, a settled course of procedure which, in its last days, was described by William Hudson in a very readable book. Its procedure, the main feature of which was the examination of the accused, perished with it. After the Civil War and the Restoration no attempt was made to revive it, but that it had been doing useful things then became evident. The old criminal law had been exceedingly defective, especially in relation to those offences which did not attain the rank of felonies. The King's Bench had, for the future, to do what the Star Chamber had done, but to do it in a more regular fashion, and not without the interposition of a jury.

Court of Chancery. Far other were the fortunes of the Star Chamber's twin sister, the Court of Chancery. Twin sisters they were; indeed, in the fourteenth century it is hard to tell one from the other, and even in the Stuart time we sometimes find the Star Chamber doing things which we should have expected to be done by the chancery. But, to go back to the fourteenth century, the chancellor was the king's first minister, the head of the one great secretarial department that there was, the president of the council, and the most learned member of the council. Usually he was a bishop; often he had earned his see by diligent labours as a clerk in the chancery. It was natural that the lords of the council should put off upon him, or that he should take to himself, a great deal of the judicial work that in one way or another the council had to do. Criminal cases might come before the whole body, or some committee of it. Throughout the Middle Ages criminal cases were treated as simple affairs; for example, justices of the peace who were not trained lawyers could be trusted to do a great deal of penal justice, and inflict the punishment of death. But cases involving civil rights, involving the complex land law, might come before the council. Generally, in such cases, there was some violence or some fraud to be complained of, some violence or fraud for which, so the complainant alleged, he could get no redress elsewhere. Such cases came specially under the eye of the chancellor. He was a learned man with learned subordinates, the masters of the chancery. Very gradually it became the practice for complainants who were seeking the reparation of wrongs rather than the punishment of offences, to address their petitions, not to the king and council, but to the chancellor. Slowly men began to think of the chancellor, or the Chancery of which he was president, as having a jurisdiction distinct from, though it might overlap, that of the council.

Its Jurisdiction. What was to be the sphere of this jurisdiction? For a long time this question remained doubtful. The wrongs of which men usually complained to the chancellor were wrongs well enough known to the common law—deeds of violence, assaults, land-grabbing, and so forth. As an excuse for going to him, they urged that they were poor while their adversaries were mighty, too mighty for the common law, with its long delays and its purchasable juries. Odd though this may seem to us, that court which was to become a byword for costly delay started business as an expeditious and a poor man's court. It met with much opposition: the House of Commons did not like it, and the common lawyers did not like it; but still there was a certain half-heartedness in the opposition. No one was prepared to say that there was no place for such a tribunal; no one was prepared to define by legislation what its place should be.

From the field of the common law the chancellor was slowly compelled to retreat. It could not be suffered that, merely because there was helplessness on the one side and corruptive wealth on the other, he should be suffered to deal with cases which belonged to the old courts. It seems possible that this nascent civil jurisdiction of the chancellor would have come to naught but for a curious episode in the history of our land law. In the second half of the fourteenth century many causes were conspiring to induce the landholders of England to convey their lands to friends, who, while becoming the legal owners of those lands, would,

nevertheless, be bound by an honourable under-
standing as to the uses to which their ownership
should be put. There were feudal burdens that
could thus be evaded, ancient restrictions which
could thus be loosened. The chancellor began
to hold himself out as willing to enforce these
honourable understandings, these "uses, trusts,
or confidences," as they were called, to send to
prison the trustee who would not keep faith.

It is an exceedingly curious episode. The whole
nation seems to enter into one large conspiracy to
evade its own laws, to evade laws which it has not the
courage to reform. The Chancellor, the Judges, and
the Parliament seem all to be in the conspiracy.
And yet there is really no conspiracy: men are but
living from hand to mouth, arguing from one case to
the next case, and they do not see what is going to
happen. Too late the king, the one person who had
steadily been losing by the process, saw what had
happened. Henry VIII. put into the mouth of a
reluctant Parliament a statute which did its best—
a clumsy best it was—to undo the work.[1] But past
history was too strong even for that high and mighty
prince. The statute was a miserable failure. A little
trickery with words would circumvent it. The
chancellor, with the active connivance of the

---

[1] *Statute of Uses* (27 Hen. VIII., c. 10). For text, see Digby, *Hist. of Law of Real Property*, 3d ed., 303-10.

judges, was enabled to do what he had been doing in the past, to enforce the obligations known as trusts.

This elaborate story we can only mention by the way; the main thing that we have to notice is that, long before the Tudor days—indeed, before the fourteenth century was out—the chancellor had acquired for himself a province of jurisdiction which was, in the opinion of all men, including the common lawyers, legitimately his own. From time to time he would extend its boundaries, and from time to time there would be a brisk quarrel between the Chancery and the law courts over the annexation of some field fertile of fees. In particular, when the chancellor forbade a man to sue in a court of law, or to take advantage of a judgment that he had obtained in a court of law, the judges resented this, and a bitter dispute about this matter between Coke and Ellesmere gave King James I. a wished-for opportunity of posing as the supreme lord of all the justice that was done in his name and awarding a decisive victory to his chancellor.[1] But such disputes were rare. The chancellors had found useful work to do, and they had been suffered to do it without much opposition. In the name of equity

[1] Case of Commendams, (1616) (Colt v. Bishop of Lichfield, Hobart 193). For brief statement of this case, see Taswell-Langmead, *Eng. Consti. Hist.*, 427–9.

and good conscience they had, as it were, been adding an appendix to the common law. Every jot and tittle of the law was to be fulfilled, and yet, when a man had done this, more might be required of him in the name of equity and good conscience.

Equity. Where were the rules of equity and good conscience to be found? Some have supposed that the clerical chancellors of the last middle ages found them in the Roman or the canon law, and certain it is that they borrowed the main principles of their procedure from the canonists. Indeed, until some reforms that are still very recent, the procedure of the Court of Chancery was the procedure of an Ecclesiastical Court. In flagrant contrast to the common law, it forced the defendant to answer on oath the charges that were brought against him; it made no use of the jury; the evidence consisted of written affidavits. On the other hand, it is by no means certain that more than this was borrowed.

So far as we can now see, the chancellors seem to get most of their dominant ideas from the common law. They imitate the common law whenever they can, and depart from it reluctantly at the call of natural justice and common honesty. Common honesty requires that a man shall observe the trust that has been committed to him. If the common law will not enforce this obligation it is failing to do its duty. The chancellor intervenes, but in enforcing trusts he seizes hold of and adopts every analogy that the common law presents. For a long time English equity seems to live from hand to mouth. Sufficient for the day are the cases in that day's cause-list. Even in the seventeenth century men said that the real measure of equity was the length of the chancellor's foot. Under the Tudors the volume of litigation that flowed into the Chancery was already enormous; the chancellor was often sadly in arrear of his work, and yet very rarely were his decisions reported, though the decisions of the judges had been reported ever since the days of Edward I. This shows us that he did not conceive himself to be straitly bound by precedents: he could still listen to the voice of conscience. The rapid increase in the number of causes that he had to decide began to make his conscience a technical conscience. More and more of his time was spent upon the judgment-seat. Slowly he ceased to be, save in ceremonial rank, the king's first minister. Wolsey was the last chancellor who ruled England (1515–29). Secretaries of state were now intervening between the king and his great seal. Its holder was destined to become year by year more of a judge, less of a statesman. Still we must look forward to the Restoration for the age in which the rules of equity begin to take a very definite shape, comparable in rigour to the rules of the common law.[1]

Somehow or other England, after a fashion all her own, had stumbled into a scheme for the reconciliation of permanence with progress. The old mediæval criminal law could be preserved because a Court of Star Chamber would supply its deficiencies; the old private law could be preserved because the Court of Chancery was composing an appendix to it; trial by jury could be preserved, developed, transfigured because other modes of trial were limiting it to an appropriate sphere. And so our old law maintained its continuity. As we have said above, it passed scatheless through the critical sixteenth century, and was ready to stand up against tyranny in the seventeenth. The Star Chamber and the Chancery were dangerous to our political liberties. Bacon could tell King James that the Chancery was the court of his absolute power. But if we look abroad we shall find good reason for thinking that but for these institutions our old-fashioned national law, unable out of its own resources to meet the requirements of a new age, would have utterly broken down, and the "ungodly jumble" would have made

[1] For explanation of the growing rigidity of the rules of equity, see Markby, *Elements of Law*, pars. 121-2; for opinion of different chancellors respecting principles by which they were guided, see Holland, *Elements of Juris.*, 69-70, and Lord Eldon, in Gee *v.* Pritchard, 2 Swanston, 414.

way for Roman jurisprudence and for despotism. Were we to say that that equity saved the common law, and that the Court of Star Chamber saved the constitution, even in this paradox there would be some truth.

READINGS

On Omnipotence of Parliament:
> Smith, Thomas, *Commonwealth of Eng.*, bk. ii., ch. ii.; Blackstone, *Com.*, I., 91 and 161; Dicey, *Law of the Consti.*, bk. i., ch. i.; Pollock, *First Book on Juris.*, pt. ii., ch. iii.

On Common Law and Statute:
> Blackstone, *Com.*, I., 61–92; Robinson, W. C., *Elements of Amer. Juris.*, ch. viii.; Ilbert, *Legislative Methods and Forms*, ch. i.; Wambaugh, E., *Study of Cases*, ch. viii.

On the Working and Development of the Common Law in the XIVth and XVth Centuries:
> Holdsworth, *Hist. of Eng. Law*, II., 338–50.

On the Growth of the Legal Profession and the Inns of Court:
> P. and M., *Hist. of Eng. Law*, I., 211–17; Holdsworth, *Hist. of Eng. Law*, I., ch. v., and II., 261–6; Dillon, *Laws and Juris. of Eng. and Amer.*, Lectures ii. and iii.; Fortescue, *De Laudibus Legum Angliæ*, ch. xlix.; Pearce, *Inns of Court*.

On the House of Lords:
> Stubbs, *Consti. Hist. of Eng.*, II., 255–60; Taswell-Langmead, *Eng. Consti. Hist.*, 150–1, and ch. xvii., pt. ii.; Medley, *Eng. Consti. Hist.*, 124–45; Carter, *Hist. of Eng. Legal Insti.*, ch. xii.

On the Star Chamber:
> Stephens, *Hist. of Crim. Law in Eng.*, I., 168–80 and 337–46; Carter, *Hist. of Eng. Legal Insti.*, ch. xiv.; Taswell-Langmead, *Eng. Consti. Hist.*, 152–4, 465–7, and 482–5; Medley, *Eng. Consti. Hist.*, 86–9 and *passim*.

On Origin and Growth of the Court of Chancery and its Jurisdiction:
> P. and M., *Hist. of Eng. Law*, I., 193–7; Spence, *Equitable Juris. of*

Court of Chancery, I., pt. ii., bk. i., chaps. i.–iv., reprinted in *Anglo-Am. Legal Hist.*, II., ch. xxviii.; Pollock, *First Book on Juris.*, 243–5, and *Expansion of the Common Law*, 66–74; Robinson, W. C., *Elements of Amer. Juris.*, 300–8; Carter, *Hist. of Eng. Legal Insti.*, ch. xv.; Bispham, *Principles of Equity*, 4th ed., 1887, Introduction and ch. i.; Taswell-Langmead, *Eng. Consti. Hist.*, 145–50; Medley, *Eng. Consti. Hist.*, 339–44.

CHAPTER VI

Completion of the Common Law and Statutory Reforms after the Restoration, 1600–1688

The Development of Law. The Restoration may be said to open a new period in the history of English law. The supremacy of the common law had been vindicated by the Long Parliament. The extraordinary courts established by the Tudors to be the bulwarks of personal government had been overthrown. The ecclesiastical courts had been reduced to dignified impotence. The Court of Chancery ceased to be an instrument of the Royal prerogative. Henceforth it was to owe the amplitude of its jurisdiction to the needs of the subject, not to the ambition of the monarch. It is true that when the monarchy had been overthrown men went on to canvass the defects of the law of England. A comprehensive reform of the law, especially of the rules of procedure, was frequently demanded in the time of the Commonwealth. But with the Restoration projects of this kind were laid aside. Tired of change and confusion, men were glad to return to the institutions of their forefathers. Satisfied to be rid for ever of the Court of Star Chamber, and the Court of High Commission, they regarded little the barbarity of the criminal law, or the vexatious expense and delay of proceedings in Chancery.

Completion of the Common Law. The common law had taken its permanent shape; its principles had been ascertained and fixed in a multitude of reported cases.[1] That minute portion of our immense legal literature which enjoys an authority comparable with the authority of judicial decisions received some of its latest and most valuable additions in the writings of the celebrated Sir Matthew Hale,[2] who held under Charles II. the offices of Chief Baron of the Exchequer and Chief Justice of the King's Bench. But the virtual completion of the common law gave fresh importance to the agencies

[1] "Up to the year 1648 there were no reports in print that I recall, but certain of the Year Books, Plowden, Dyer, Keilway, Benloe, and Dalison in Ashe, the first eleven parts of Coke, Davies, Hobart, and Bellewe's Collections out of the Abridgments. But now 'came forth,' says an historian of the time, 'a flying squadron of thin Reports.' . . . Up to the year 1776, the whole number of Reports in England, both at law and equity, did not much exceed a hundred and fifty volumes, while in the United States there was not then, nor for many years afterwards, so much as a single one."—Wallace, *The Reporters*, 4th ed., 1882, 7 and 24.

[2] For sketch of his life, see Campbell, *Lives of the Chief Justices of England*, II., chaps. xvi., xvii., xviii.; Foss, *The Judges of England*, 319-22.

by which it could be supplemented or improved.
From this time forwards the adaptation of law to the
needs of society is carried on chiefly by the Courts of
Equity and by the Legislature.

Independence of the Jury. One momentous
reform, indeed, is due to a judicial decision given in
this period. The independence of jurors was secured
by the famous judgment in Bushell's case. That
jurors might be called to account for giving a verdict
against the weight of evidence and the direction of
the Court was too convenient a doctrine not to find
acceptance with the Tudor sovereigns. They did not
hesitate to mark their displeasure with jurors who
had returned a verdict contrary to their wishes. The
offenders were liable to be reprimanded by the
judges, or to be summoned before the Star Chamber,
which was usually content to admonish, but sometimes visited them with fine or imprisonment.[1]
These precedents were not forgotten under the
Stuarts. Even after the abolition of the Star Chamber, jurors were occasionally rebuked or fined by the
Chief Justice of the King's Bench. With the decline
of personal government, however, this practice called
down more and more general disapproval. In 1667
the House of Commons formally condemned it by
resolution. A little later all the judges, save one,
agreed in declaring that it was unlawful to fine

[1] See Throckmorton's Case, 1554, I., State Trials, 869.

jurors for returning a verdict against the direction of the Court.

Bushell's Case. The last person fined for this offence was Edward Bushell, one of the jury which in 1670 acquitted the Quakers Penn and Mead, when indicted before the Recorder of the City of London for having held an unlawful assembly. As the verdict was against the Recorder's direction, he fined each of the jurors forty marks, and, on Bushell's refusing to pay, committed him to custody. Bushell sued out his habeas corpus. Vaughan, Chief Justice of the Common Pleas, held that the ground of his committal was insufficient, and set him at liberty. Since that time no juryman has been called in question for giving a verdict according to his own judgment.

Equity. The history of modern equity begins with the reign of Charles II. Not only was the Court of Chancery more recent in its origin than the Courts of Common Law, but it was remarkably slow to form a definite jurisprudence. This may have been due partly to the auxiliary nature of its jurisdiction, and partly to the fact that the chancellor was a great officer of State, who had been promoted for qualities distinct from those of the professional lawyer, who had many other things to do besides administering justice, and who was much more deeply concerned in urgent matters of civil and ecclesiastical policy than in giving a systematic form to his corrections of the ancient law. The rules of equity could not be methodized until the chancellor should regard the dispensation of equity as his principal function and the office of chancellor should be given only to men who had made the law their profession. But these changes took many years to effect.

Lawyers as Chancellors. The last clerical Lord Keeper was Williams, Bishop of Lincoln, who held the Great Seal from 1622 to 1625. The last chancellor who could be termed the chief adviser of the Crown was Lord Clarendon. The last chancellor who was not a lawyer by profession was his successor, Lord Shaftesbury. Dryden has varied his invective against Shaftesbury as a statesman by praising Shaftesbury as a judge. It seems probable, however, that the satire was better merited than the panegyric. The third chancellor of Charles II., Sir Heneage Finch (afterwards Earl of Nottingham), is the beginner of a new era. A jurist first, and a public man afterwards, he owes his high place among the chancellors of England solely to his transcendent merits as a judge. He is the first in that series of great magistrates by whom equity was reduced to a system almost as precise and as little dependent upon individual opinion as the common law itself, the first to take away the reproach that equity had no measure out the chancellor's foot.[1]   But he was less fortunate than his successors in the circumstance that his decisions were ill-reported.

Statute Law. More generally intelligible and interesting than the fixing of the rules of equity is the legislation which signalizes the period between the Restoration and the Revolution. Compared with earlier legislation, it is remarkably copious. The statutes of Charles II. surpass in bulk the statutes of every previous reign, except the reign of Henry VIII. Several are of the highest importance. Among them may be noted the Statute of Distributions, which first established a reasonable rule for the administration of the personalty of those dying intestate.[2]

Statute of Frauds. Still more noteworthy is the Statute of Frauds, passed—as the preamble informs

[1] "When the benefit of the King's equity was once a matter of right, it was inevitable that the rules of equity should become as methodical as any other part of the law. Blackstone could already say with truth that 'the system of our courts of equity is a laboured connected system, governed by established rules and bound down by precedents.' "—Pollock, *First Book on Juris.*, 244.

[2] The old law *de rationabile parte bonorum* was confirmed, in regard to the goods of intestates, by the Statute of Distributions (22, 23 Car. II., c. 10) which directed that, after the payment of all just debts of the intestate, the surplusage was to be distributed in the following manner: To the widow one-third, and to the children or their representatives an equal share; and if there were no children, then one-half to the widow, and the other half equally to the next of kin of the intestate; and if there were neither widow nor children, then the whole in equal shares to the next of kin. See Blackstone, *Com.*, II., 515.

us—"for prevention of many fraudulent practices which are commonly endeavoured to be upheld by perjury and subornation of perjury." With this object it required a written form for certain classes of contracts, leases, and wills. Whether it has accomplished its purpose, or ' accomplished that purpose in the best way, is still disputed. What is certain is, that no other Act of Parliament has given rise to so much litigation.[1] But even the Statute of Frauds and the Statute of Distributions yield in importance to the memorable enactments which abolished tenures in chivalry and assured the personal freedom of the subject. These enactments claim separate notice.

Military Tenures. These tenures were definitely established in England as a part of his feudalizing policy by the Conqueror. Although the incidents of these tenures had been modified from time to time by his successors they had never effectually fulfilled their purpose of providing the Crown with a trustworthy military force. Personal service was commuted for the money payment known as scutage, and scutage came to be less and less productive as a source of revenue. It had long been replaced by other forms of taxation on land, when Charles I. thought of reviving it in 1640 in order to supply the immediate

[1] For explanation see art. on the "Statute of Frauds," by Sir J. F. Stephen in *Law Quar. Rev.*, I., 6, Jan., 1885.

necessities of the war against the Scotch Covenanters. But the incidents of military tenure, other than the obligation to military service, remained, and appeared all the more burdensome now that they were no longer justified by circumstances.

Among such incidents the most unreasonable and the most oppressive were the rights of wardship and marriage. Originally, even these rights might have been justified. So long as the tenant holding directly from the Crown was a military chief, the Crown had some ground for claiming the guardianship of his infant heir. If he left an heiress, the Crown might not unfairly claim a voice in choosing the husband to whom she would transfer the command of her vassals. And the rights which the Crown claimed over its tenants in chief were naturally claimed by them over their military tenants. But when the holder of land on military tenure had lost his military character, it was intolerable that he should not be able to choose a guardian for his children, and that the Crown should maladminister his estate if he died before they came of age. It was even more intolerable that, if he left an heiress, the Crown should interfere with her choice of a husband.

Oppressive in themselves as were the rights of wardship and marriage, they were aggravated by the abuses of the Court of Wards established in the reign of Henry VIII. The loss to the military tenants was

great, and the gain to the Crown was small. From
the accession of the Stuarts, the commutation of the
incidents of military tenure for a fixed hereditary revenue to be settled on the king had been a cherished
scheme of reform. An agreement to that effect
known as the Great Contract had been set on foot
between James I. and his Parliament, but had not
been concluded because James thought that the
annual sum of £200,000 offered by the House of
Commons was not an adequate consideration. In
the course of the negotiations with Parliament,
opened in 1648, and known as the Treaty of Newport,
Charles I. offered to accept a revenue of £100,000 in
lieu of his rights over the military tenants. It is true
that the military tenures had already been abolished
by an ordinance of the Parliament. During the
Commonwealth this ordinance held good, and when
Charles II. returned to England, it was found impossible to revive a set of abuses which had been
suspended for fifteen years.

Their Abolition. The Convention Parliament
therefore passed the famous Act, 12 Car. II., c. 24,
taking away the Courts of Wards and all the incidents of military tenure or tenure in chivalry. All
the land hitherto held upon this tenure was hence-
forward to be held in free and common socage, a
tenure involving merely nominal services. In compensation for the revenues thus taken away, the

king received a hereditary excise upon beer and other liquors. It is a mistake to imagine that the nation lost anything by the abolition of the military tenures. Personal service had long been out of date, and all pecuniary payments, having become fixed at a remote period, had become insignificant through the fall in the value of the precious metals.

Effect on Landed Property. By this Act the power of devising land by will was indirectly enlarged. That power had virtually disappeared on the completion of the feudal system. A statute of the thirty-second year of Henry VIII. (1540) had empowered a tenant in fee simple to dispose by will of all his land held in socage, but of only two-thirds of his land held in chivalry. Now that tenure in chivalry was converted into tenure in socage, the tenant in fee simple could dispose by his will of all lands whatsoever.

This Act also gave every father power to appoint a guardian to his children, and gave the guardian full control over the ward's estate, both real and personal. Formerly, when a socage tenant left an heir under age, the next of kin who could not inherit the land became his guardian irrespective of the father's wishes. Lastly, this Act deprived the Crown of the celebrated rights of purveyance and pre-emption. In virtue of these rights the king's officers had been accustomed to take supplies for his household practically at prices fixed by their own discretion. The incessant movements and vast retinue of our mediæval kings had made these rights the means of endless loss and vexation to the subject. To restrain the abuse of these rights had been the object of a long series of unavailing enactments, beginning with Magna Carta. In conclusion, it may be said that the Act for taking away the military tenures completed the ruin of the feudal land-law. The numerous fragments of feudalism which remain embedded in the modern law of real property are, for the most part, insignificant.

Habeas Corpus. In comparison with the Act which swept away so much of the common law, an Act which merely improved the procedure for enforcing a single common-law right might seem trivial. But that right was most precious of all, the right to personal freedom, and the statute which rendered it secure, although generally misunderstood, has not been prized too dearly. The right not to be imprisoned save on grounds defined by law, and, if imprisoned on a criminal charge, to be brought to trial within a reasonable time, is far older than the Habeas Corpus Act, and is, indeed, asserted in general terms in the thirty-ninth clause of Magna Carta, by which the king undertakes that no free man shall be imprisoned otherwise than by the lawful judgment of his peers, or by the law of the land.

A person detained in prison was entitled under the common law to demand from the Court of King's Bench a writ of *habeas corpus ad subjiciendum* (*i. e.*, have the body to submit to the court) addressed to the person who had him in custody. The gaoler then had to produce him in court, together with the warrant for his commitment. The Court had authority to inquire into the sufficiency of the warrant, and either to discharge the prisoner or to admit him to bail, or to send him back to prison. It should be added that the Court had no discretion to refuse the writ. In practice, however, these legal securities proved insufficient. Sincere belief in the necessity of state, or timid subservience to the king often led the judges to decline making any order on the writ.

Means of communication were so imperfect that a prisoner once removed to some distant place of confinement might languish there for years before any friend (if he had friends) could discover where he was. If a prisoner were conveyed out of the kingdom of England he was beyond the jurisdiction of the King's Bench, and had no legal remedy for his detention. Lastly, the procedure was subject to technical defects. It was doubtful whether the writ of habeas corpus could be issued by the Court of Common Pleas or by the Court of Exchequer, and whether a single judge could issue it during vacation.

Under these circumstances, it is not surprising that cases of arbitrary imprisonment frequently occurred down to the meeting of the Long Parliament. Even after the Restoration, Clarendon, who preserved the traditions of the old monarchy, offended several times against the liberty of the subject. The House of Commons, therefore, sought to provide an effectual remedy. Bills with this intention were introduced in 1668, in 1670, in 1673, and in 1675, but it was not until 1679 that the celebrated Habeas Corpus Act (31 Car. II., c. 2) was passed with the assistance of Lord Shaftesbury.

Habeas Corpus Act. The chief provisions of this Act are as follows: It inflicted the penalties of a *præmunire* (imprisonment for life and forfeiture of goods and chattels) on every person who should send an inhabitant of England a prisoner into Scotland, or any place beyond seas (and therefore out of the jurisdiction of the Courts at Westminster). It made effectual the common-law right of every person committed on a charge of misdemeanour to be released upon giving bail for his appearance. He might apply during vacation to the chancellor, or any one of the judges, who were required, under heavy penalties, to grant him the writ of habeas corpus. Heavy penalties were also denounced against the gaoler who failed to obey the writ. The Act also provided for the case of a prisoner committed on a charge of treason or of felony. If not brought to trial at the next sittings after his commitment, he was to be set at liberty on bail, unless it were proved upon oath that the witnesses for the Crown could not then be produced. If not brought to trial at the second sittings after his committal, he was to be discharged altogether. No person set at liberty on a writ of habeas corpus was to be again imprisoned on the same charge otherwise than by order of the court having jurisdiction in his case. The very fact that in troubled times, when it may be necessary to imprison persons whom it is inconvenient to try, the Legislature has been compelled to suspend this statute, is enough to prove that the securities which it provides are real and substantial.

Burning of Heretics. Less important in its bearing on practice, but hardly less interesting to the historian, is the Act of 1677, which abolished the punishment of death for the offence of heresy. Considerable uncertainty hangs over the origin of the famous *writ de hæretico comburendo*, under which so many persons were burnt alive for their religious opinions. Ever since the conversion of England to Christianity heretics had been subject to ecclesiastical penalties. Sir Matthew Hale asserted in his *Pleas of the Crown* that the common law recognized a writ under which heretics might be burned. But Mr. Justice Stephen, in his *History of the Criminal Law*, doubts the exis-

tence of any such writ at common law, on the ground
that there is no instance of its having been issued
previous to the year 1400.

Be this as it may, an Act of that year (2 Hen. IV.,
c. 15) required the sheriffs to burn to death the
obstinate heretics delivered over to them by the
ecclesiastical courts. And although the law relating
to heresy was frequently modified in subsequent
times, and the last case in which heretics were burnt
occurred in the year 1612, the *writ de hæretico comburendo* was not abolished until the year 1677. An
Act of that year (29 Car. II., c. 9) puts an end to all
capital punishment in pursuance of ecclesiastical
censures, although it permits the judges of ecclesiastical courts to inflict ecclesiastical punishments such
as excommunication, deprivation, or degradation on
persons guilty of "atheism, blasphemy, heresy, or
schism, and other damnable doctrines and opinions."
Even if this Act had never been passed, it is unlikely
that any person would have suffered death for his
religious opinions. But the formal abolition of
capital punishment for heretics marks the progress
of the doctrine of religious toleration.

10

READINGS

On Independence of the Jury:
Bushell's Case, 6 State Trials, 999; Stephen, J. F., *Hist. of Crim. Law of Eng.*, I., 374–5; May, *Consti. Hist. of Eng.*, II., ch. ix. (The Press and Liberty of Opinion), *passim*; Taswell-Langmead, *Eng. Consti. Hist.*, 142–3; Medley, *Eng. Consti. Hist.*, 410–11.

On Development of Equity since 1660:
Jenks, *Short Hist. of Eng. Law*, 207–12; Campbell's *Lives of Lord Chancellors of Eng.* (Sketch of Heneage Finch—Lord Nottingham—and his work in reducing Equity to a system), vol. III., chaps. xci.–xciii.

On Statute Law, 1660–1688:
History of Military Tenures and their Abolition:
P. and M., *Hist. of Eng. Law*, I., 252–82; Blackstone, *Com.*, II., 62–77; Digby, *Hist. of the Law of Real Property*, ch. ix.; Taswell-Langmead, *Eng. Consti. Hist.*, 48–55, and 511–12; Medley, *Eng. Consti. Hist.*, ch. i., 19–27, 54.

Habeas Corpus Act and its Suspension:
Hallam, *Consti. Hist. of Eng.*, 499–502, 5th London ed., 1857; May, *Consti. Hist. of Eng.*, II., ch. xi., 245–57; Dicey, *Law of Consti.*, ch. iv.; Taswell-Langmead, *Eng. Consti. Hist.*, 518–22 and Index; Medley, *Eng. Consti. Hist.*, 390–3; Jenks, "The Story of the Habeas Corpus," *Law Quar. Rev.*, XVIII., Jan., 1902, 64–77, reprinted in *Anglo-Am. Legal Hist.*, II., ch. xxxv.

Offences against Religion and the Theory of Persecution:
Stephen, *Hist. of Crim. Law of Eng.*, II., ch. xxv.; Pollock, *Essays in Juris. and Ethics*, ch. vi.; Taswell-Langmead, *Eng. Consti. Hist.*, 522–28.

CHAPTER VII

SUPREMACY OF PARLIAMENT AND RAPID GROWTH OF STATUTE LAW, 1688–1800.

Effect of the Revolution. From the date of the Revolution the history of legal innovation becomes more and more a history of statutes. The Revolution restored unity and energy to the legislature, by subordinating the Crown to the Parliament. It put an end to the long intervals between Parliament and Parliament, and between session and session. It rendered almost impossible the abrupt prorogations and dissolutions of the seventeenth century. It made the sovereign and his ministers anxious to comply with the wishes of the nation to expedite business and to obtain by popular arts a liberal supply. It virtually deprived the sovereign of his right to reject bills which had passed both Houses. This right was indeed exercised several times by William with reference to measures of grave consequence, but it was only once exercised by Anne,[1] and has never been exercised since her

[1] This was in 1707 when she refused assent to the Scotch Militia Bill. Anson, *Law and Custom of the Consti.*, I., 287, 2d ed., 1892.

147

death. Since the Revolution Parliament has met every year, and has sat for a considerable time. The deliberate wishes of Parliament have, since the Revolution, encountered no serious opposition. Ample opportunity has thus been afforded for all the legislation demanded by public opinion, and direct legislation has thus become the normal means of altering the law. Judicial decision continues indeed to be a potent agency of improvement, but it is used rather to define and apply principles already acknowledged than to introduce principles altogether novel.

Progress of Statute Law. It is true that, except in the province of constitutional law, few important changes were effected by statute in the reigns of William III., of Anne, and of George I. A few statutes may be cited for their antiquarian interest or for their relation to the general history of the time.

Thus the abolition of the Court of the Marches of Wales (1697-8), founded by Henry VIII., effaced the last vestige of a time when Wales was still imperfectly subdued, and an extraordinary jurisdiction had been required to keep it in order. The extension of benefit of clergy[1] to women in the case of those felonies in which it had hitherto been enjoyed by men marks the completion of a long process by which benefit of clergy, once available only to clerks, and

---

[1] Benefit of clergy was abolished in 1827, 7 & 8 Geo. IV., c. 28. See reading on Benefit of Clergy at end of Ch. II.

then extended to all who could read, finally came to lose all reference to the clerical profession. The right of the owner of personal property to bequeath it as he saw fit was established throughout England. Hitherto in the ecclesiastical province of York and in the city of London custom had given the widow and children of the deceased an indefeasible right to a certain proportion of his personal estate. This custom was now abrogated in the northern province by a statute of 1692, and in London by a statute of 1724.

Merchants and traders were benefited by the Act of William III. (1697–8), which enabled them to agree that a reference to arbitration should be made a rule of court, so that the arbitrator's decision should be binding on both parties; and by the Act of Anne, which conferred upon promissory notes the character of negotiable instruments.[1] The first serious attempt since the Reformation to ensure an adequate maintenance for the inferior clergy was made by the Act of Anne, which constituted the first-fruits and tenths hitherto received by the Crown into a fund for the augmentation of the poorest livings. The prevalence of gambling in this period is indicated by a severe Act of the same reign (1710), which rendered void

[1] 3 & 4 Anne, c. 9 (1704). See Parsons, *Bills and Notes*, I., 9–13, for text of this famous act with history of the difficulties that led to its passage; also *Am. and Eng. Ency. of Law*, 1st ed., II., 314.

securities of every kind given for money lost in games or in betting on the players, or knowingly advanced for such purposes.

Reform of Trial for Treason. A more serious interest is awakened by the Act for regulating trials in cases of treason and misprision of treason. For this Act is memorable, not only in the history of the Constitution, but also in the history of English criminal procedure.

In trials for treason and felony—that is to say, in all capital causes—the common law placed the accused at a grave disadvantage. Kept in confinement until the day of his trial, he had no right to see his indictment, to be informed what witnesses would depose against him, or to confer with professional lawyers as to his defence. At the trial his witnesses were not examined upon oath as were the witnesses for the Crown. He was forced to make his own defence, although he was allowed to have a legal adviser at his side. Thus at a moment's notice, and under the apprehension of a shameful death, without legal learning, without practice in cross-examining, without training in advocacy, the miserable wretch had to contend against an indictment cunningly framed, against evidence rendered impressive by an oath, and against prosecutors whose lives were spent in constant forensic exercise. Persons accused of treason were in a position of peculiar hardship. For the judge was almost always prejudiced in favour of the Crown, the jury was too often packed by the sheriff, and the prosecuting counsel might hope to make their own careers by securing a conviction.

In the numerous trials for treason which took place between the Restoration and the Revolution, the inherent vices of the procedure were so much aggravated by the servility and brutality of the bench, as to call forth a demand for reform, especially among the Whigs, who had been the greatest sufferers. Accordingly, a bill for regulating trials in cases of treason was introduced in 1691, but was lost, partly because the Whigs, who were now in power, no longer cared to blunt the weapons of the Government; and partly because the Lords desired a larger measure of protection for their own order than the Commons cared to concede.

It was not until 1695 that the bill, brought in again and again, became law (7 William III., c. 3). It provided that a person accused of treason should have a copy of the indictment at least five days, and a copy of the panel of jurors at least two days, before trial. It gave him the right to take legal advice, to make his defence by counsel, to have his witnesses examined upon oath, and to compel their attendance by the process already available with respect to witnesses for the Crown. Two witnesses were already required, by a statute of Edward VI., for conviction on a charge of treason. The statute of William III. added that both witnesses must testify to the same overt act of treason, or one of them to one and the other to another act of the same treason. Except on the charge of attempting to assassinate the King, no person was to be indicted for treason unless within three years of the alleged offence. Finally, this Act conceded the demand of the Peers, that on the trial of a peer or peeress for treason, a summons should be sent, not, as formerly, to a small number of peers selected by the Lord High Steward, but to every peer who was entitled to sit and vote. Thus the procedure in trials for treason was rendered rational and humane.

Mr. Justice Stephen notes in his *History of the Criminal Law* that the passing of this Act seems to have had very little influence on the fate of accused persons. But it must be remembered that the governments which succeeded the Revolution were usually careful not to incur the odium of unreasonable and unnecessary prosecutions. The procedure in trials for felony remained on the bad old footing. In the course of the eighteenth century it became the custom to allow the accused the help of counsel for every purpose, except that of making the speech for the defence. This right was not conceded until 1836.[1]

[1] 6 & 7 Will. IV., c. 114. See *Century of Law Reform*, 50.

Law of Copyright. The Copyright Act of 1709[1] is a fitting legal monument of a literary age. Before the invention of printing, comparatively few copies can have been made, even of a successful and popular work. No author lived, or could have hoped to live, upon the profits derived from the sale of his writings. Even after the introduction of printing into England, a hundred years elapsed, it is said, without any legal recognition of copyright. In the seventeenth century, however, the number of readers became so considerable, that the exclusive right of printing and publishing a book might well be worth possessing. Such a right was recognized by the courts of common law. The common law copyright was in so far more valuable than the statutory copyright which authors now enjoy, that it was unlimited in point of duration. But it was practically of little benefit, because it could not be enforced. The party entitled to the copyright could recover damages to the extent of the loss which he could prove, and it was impossible for him to prove the sale of any but a few of the pirated copies. Even these damages he rarely recovered, because the defendant was usually a pauper.

Under these circumstances, persons interested in copyright were loud in their complaints. Their petitions were answered by the statute 8 Anne, c. 19,

[1] 8 Anne, c. 21.

which became the basis of all subsequent legislation. This statute provided that the author of any work printed before the 10th of April, 1710, was to have the exclusive right of publishing for twenty-one years. The author of any work printed after that date was to have the same right for fourteen years, and if he were living at the expiration of that period, the right was to be renewed to him for a similar period. All copies published in contravention of the statute were to be forfeited to the owner of the copyright, who was to reduce them to waste paper. The offending publisher was also to forfeit a penny for every sheet of pirated matter in his possession.

Lest any bookseller should be able to plead ignorance as an excuse for breaking the law, the person having copyright was required to record his title in the register book of the Stationers' Company, which was to be open to inspection by the public. In order that booksellers might not demand an unreasonable price for publications in which they had copyright, the Act allowed complaint to be made to the Archbishop of Canterbury, to the Lord Keeper, and to certain other dignitaries, and gave them power to limit the price as, upon inquiry, they should think reasonable. It would be interesting to know whether advantage was ever taken of this curious provision. Lastly, the Act required nine copies of every new book to be delivered at Stationers' Hall, for the use

of certain libraries.[1] For a long time it was supposed
that the copyright conferred by the Act of Anne did
not affect the perpetual copyright recognized by the
common law.   But in the case of Donaldson *v.*
Beckett,[2] decided in 1774, the House of Lords held
that the common law copyright had been altogether
abrogated by the Act of Anne.   That Act was in turn
repealed by the Act 5 & 6 Victoria, c. 45, (1842),
which long contained the modern law of copyright.

[The present state of the law upon this subject is
described by Jenks, as follows:

"The Copyright Act, 1911" (1 & 2 Geo. V., c. 46),
which supersedes for most purposes all previous
legislation on the subject, "deals with all its as-
pects, national, colonial, and international; also, in
addition to books and other printed matter, with
dramatic work, artistic work (pictures, sculptures,
and architectural drawings), engravings, and photo-
graphs. The chief changes introduced by it are, to
fix a uniform period for copyright of the author's life,
and fifty years further, or, where the work is posthu-
mously published, of fifty years from publication.
. . . The new statute substantially incorporates the
provisions of the existing International Copyright
Acts, by empowering the Crown to extend their

[1] The royal library, the libraries of the Universities of Oxford and
Cambridge, the libraries of the Scotch Universities, the library of
Sion College, London, and the Advocates' Library, Edinburgh.

[2] 4 Burr, 2408.

operation to such countries as shall have made due provision for reciprocal treatment of British authors; but the operation of such an Order will not extend to a self-governing colony, unless the colony voluntarily adopts it. Similarly, the Copyright Act itself, though generally operative throughout the Empire, will not apply to a self-governing colony; unless such colony has enacted satisfactory provisions for the protection of British authors within its boundaries, or unless the legislature of such colony has expressly adopted it."]—*Short Hist. of Eng. Law*, 281-3.

Registration of Title. The establishment of the Middlesex and Yorkshire registries of documents affecting the title to land in those counties deserves a brief notice here. The publicity of all dealings with land is so obviously desirable that many attempts have been made to secure it in England. The ancient ceremony known as livery of seisin had, to some extent, secured this object so long as livery of seisin was essential to a conveyance of lands. When the lawyers had contrived to evade the necessity of livery of seisin, an Act of Henry VIII. required every bargain and sale of freehold lands to be enrolled (*i. e.*, registered) either in one of the courts at Westminster or in the county where the lands were situated. But ingenious lawyers soon discovered a means of evading this statute, so that transfers of land again became secret, and the bad effects of secrecy were experienced once more. In the seventeenth century the remedy of registration was frequently suggested. Bills for the registration of transactions relating to land were introduced under the Commonwealth, but failed to become law. After the Restoration a committee of the House of Lords reported that the widespread uncertainty of title was a prime cause of the depreciation of landed property, and that this uncertainty might be cured by a system of registration. Registration was again recommended by Chamberlayne, one of the best known projectors and pamphleteers of the time of William III. Under Queen Anne registries were actually established in the East and West Ridings of Yorkshire and in Middlesex.

These registries were, in technical language, registries of assurances, not of title. In other words, they contained a record, not of the actual owners of the land, but of all transactions affecting the land. An intending purchaser or mortgagee would have found, upon searching them, no direct information as to the person entitled to deal with the estate which attracted him, but a mass of evidence from which he might infer for himself who was the person so entitled. An Act of 1735 established a similar registry of assurances in the North Riding, and an Act of 1884 consolidated and amended the law relating to the Yorkshire registries. But the system of registration devised for Yorkshire and Middlesex in the reign of Anne has never been applied to any other county. Perhaps this fact may be taken to prove that it is inadequate to the needs of modern society.[1]

A memorable concession was made to common sense by the Act of the fourth year of George II., which provided that from the 25th of March, 1733, all writs, pleadings, indictments, patents, charters, pardons, etc., and all proceedings in any court of justice in England, should be in the English language only, and not in French or Latin. Two years later the provisions of this Act were declared to apply to all courts in Wales.

A concession alike to humanity and to common sense was made by the Act of 1736 repealing the old statutes against witchcraft and forbidding any prosecution to be instituted for that offence.[2] Less interesting, but of some importance to our law of real property is the Act of 9 George II., c. 36, which

---

[1] For provisions of the new land transfer acts, 1862–97, and compulsory registration of titles, see *Century of Law Reform*, 324–40.

The Acts of 1862 and 1875 were not compulsory, but the Act of 1897 (Halsbury's Act) contained provisions for gradually making the registration of titles compulsory throughout England on the occasion of sale. Thus far, however, only the County of London has been prescribed, pursuant to the provisions of that Act, a compulsory area, and registration of titles elsewhere is still voluntary and, in fact, seldom made. See Jenks, *Short Hist. of Eng. Law*, 259–60.

[2] For history of law and trials for witchcraft in Eng., see Stephen, *Hist. of Crim. Law of Eng.*, I., 54; II., 410, 430–6. See also Thayer, J. B., *Legal Essays*, ch. xii., Trial by Jury of Things Supernatural.

avoided any gift to charitable uses of land or of
money to be laid out in buying land unless made by a
deed executed in presence of witnesses, at least twelve
months before the death of the donor, and enrolled in
the Court of Chancery within six months of execu-
tion.   This Act is sometimes termed the Mortmain
Act of George II.; but the name is hardly accurate,
since its object was not to prevent charitable gifts of
land, but to prevent the soliciting of such gifts from
men on their death-bed.   It was repealed by the
Mortmain and Charitable Uses Act of 1888, which
has in turn been altered by an Act of 1891.   Testamentary gifts of land to charitable uses are now valid,
but the land must, as a rule, be sold within a year of
the death of the testator.

READINGS

On Effect of the Revolution of 1688 upon the Law:
12 Car. II., c. 12 (1660), confirming judicial proceedings with specified exceptions since the 1st of May, 1642; Pollock, *Essays in Juris. and Ethics*, ch. viii., 228–33.

On Meaning and History of the Veto Power of the Crown and its Present Residuary Power in Legislation:
Anson, *Law and Custom of the Consti.*, 2d ed., 1892, I., 9, 32, 285; Dicey, *Law of the Consti.*, 26, n., 107, 109, 111, 116; Burgess, *Pol. Sci. and Consti. Law*, II., 76, 200–3.

On History of the Law of Treason:
Stephen, *Hist. of Crim. Law of Eng.*, II., ch. xxiii., Cases of Treason, 1660–1760, and I., 369–427; Holdsworth, *Hist. of Eng. Law*, II., 372–4; Hallam, *Consti. Hist. of Eng.*, 574–86, 5th London ed., 1857; May, *Consti. Hist. of Eng.*, II., chaps. ix., x. *passim;* Taswell-Langmead, *Eng. Consti. Hist.*, 230, note, and *passim.*

On History of the Copyright Act of 1709 and its Amendments with Provisions of Copyright Act, 1911, now in Force:
Jenks, *Short Hist. of Eng. Law*, 276–83.

On Provisions of the New Land Transfer Acts, 1862–97, and of the Act of 1897 for Compulsory Registration of Titles in Certain Specified Areas:
Century of Law Reform, 324–40; Jenks, *Short Hist. of Eng. Law*, 255–61.

CHAPTER VIII

GROWTH OF STATUTE LAW AND LEGAL REFORMS IN THE NINETEENTH CENTURY

History of Law in the Nineteenth Century. In our legal history the nineteenth century is pre-eminently the period of direct legislation. The development of custom or of a traditional equity by judicial decision is at best a slow and irregular process, and it has its limits. A time comes when all the important deductions which can be drawn from an accepted principle have been exhausted. Further growth will then involve a transformation of the principle itself to which judicial authority is inadequate. The main outlines of our Common Law have been settled for some hundreds of years. The main outlines of Equity were settled before the end of the last century. The critical spirit of modern times necessarily restricts the latitude of interpretation enjoyed by judges. Yet the circumstances of our age have necessitated immense changes in the law.

Growth of Statute Law. The writings of Bentham

and his school and the example of foreign nations have called forth the desire for comprehensive and symmetrical legislation. The reformed Parliaments, at least before the recent unprecedented growth of loquacity, have been eager for work and fairly capable of doing business. Thus every year has produced a volume of statutes. Some of these statutes exceed in bulk the whole legislation of a mediæval reign.[1] It would be impossible in our limits to give even a curt analysis of even one or two of these statutes, such as the Merchant Shipping Act of 1894, or the Conveyancing Act of 1881. We can only indicate the subjects with which legislation has been chiefly conversant, and the tendencies which legislation has displayed.

Public Law and Procedure. A great part of our modern statutes has been concerned with what it is convenient to call public law. Not only has the governing authority in the State been remodelled by Reform Acts and Acts for the Redistribution of Seats, but old departments of administration have

[1] "The conquerors of Crecy (1346) looked with undisguised alarm at any new project of law, and the fact that a reform necessitated a new statute was an admitted and often a fatal obstacle to its success. All the volumes of our statutes, from their beginning under Henry III. (1216–72) to the close of the reign of George II. (1760) do not equal the quantity of legislative work done in a decade of any subsequent reign."—Hearn, *Legal Duties and Rights*, 21.

For differences between ordinances and statutes and preference of early parliaments for the former, see Taswell-Langmead, *Eng. Consti. Hist.*, 230–1.

been reorganized, new departments have been established, and the entire system of local government has been recast. Here we need consider only those enactments which have altered the constitution of the courts of justice and the forms of procedure. There have been many such enactments in the nineteenth century. The whole administration of justice has been revised more than once: ancient courts have been transformed, new courts have been multiplied, and the rules of procedure have been amended again and again. We may consider first the civil and then the criminal courts, and in each case we may consider the superior courts first.

Common Law Courts. With regard to the Courts of Common Law the first notable change in this century was the suppression of the separate Welsh judicature. Formerly there had been eight Welsh judges, inferior in dignity to the judges of the courts at Westminster, but discharging similar functions within the Principality. These judgeships were abolished by an Act of 1830[1] which added one puisne judge to each of the three superior Courts of Common Law. The procedure of the Courts of Common Law was amended and simplified by statutes of 1852, 1854, and 1860, which are known as the Common Law Procedure Acts.

Courts of Equity. In the Court of Chancery, at

---

[1] See *Century of Law Reform*, 230–1.

the beginning of the nineteenth century, justice was dispensed by the Chancellor and the Master of the Rolls acting as judges of first instance, and an appeal lay only to the House of Lords. The increase of business led to the appointment of a Vice-Chancellor in 1813. Two more Vice-Chancellors were appointed in 1841 on the suppression of the equity side of the Common Law Court of Exchequer. In the year 1851 there was interposed between the House of Lords and the Court of Chancery the Court of the Lords Justices of Appeal in Chancery. Down to the passing of the first Judicature Act the procedure of the Courts of Equity had not been much modified by legislation.

Probate and Divorce. The jurisdiction in testamentary and matrimonial causes had remained to the Ecclesiastical Courts until the year 1857, when it was transferred to the lay courts, newly established. Power to pronounce a total divorce between man and wife was now first given to a court of justice. The new Court of Probate and the new Court for Divorce and Matrimonial Causes inherited much of the substantive law and procedure in use with their predecessors, and derived from the canon or the civil law. Although secular, they, with the older Court of Admiralty, formed a group apart from the Courts of Common Law and the Courts of Equity.

The Judicature Act, 1873. Thus in spite of many

considerable modifications the superior courts of justice preserved down to the year 1873 the same general outline which they had received in the thirteenth and fourteenth centuries. In that year was passed the first and most important of the Judicature Acts, which have transformed our courts and our procedure. The Judicature Act of 1873 was intended to effect three objects. It was to combine in one system the superior courts already existing; to compound a new procedure out of all that was best in the old procedure, whether of the Courts of Common Law or of the Courts of Equity, and to effect a fusion of the substantive rules of Equity with those of the Common Law.

Courts before the Act. At the passing of this Act the list of the superior courts was as follows. There were three superior Courts of Common Law—the Queen's Bench, the Common Pleas, and the Exchequer. From each of these courts an appeal lay to the Court of Exchequer Chamber, composed of all the Common Law judges except those belonging to the court where the case had been heard in the first instance. From the Court of Exchequer Chamber a final appeal lay to the House of Lords. There was, strictly speaking, but one Court of Chancery, though there were several Chancery judges. From the Court of Chancery an appeal lay to the Lords Justices of Appeal, and thence to the House of Lords.

Distinct from the Courts of Common Law and of Chancery, alike in their history, in their jurisdiction, and in their procedure, stood the Court of Admiralty, the Court of Probate, and the Court for Matrimonial Causes. Appeals from the Court of Admiralty were carried to the Judicial Committee of the Privy Council. Appeals from the Courts of Probate and Divorce were carried to the House of Lords. For judicial purposes the House of Lords consisted of the Chancellor and the "law lords," that is to say, peers who had held high judicial office. These were men eminent in their profession, but often unfitted by years and infirmities for the task of judges of appeal.

All these courts were concentrated in London. To them we must add the superior courts of the Palatine Counties, the Chancery Court and Court of Common Pleas of Lancaster and the Court of Pleas at Durham.

The Courts after the Act. The Judicature Act of 1873 created a Supreme Court of Judicature, which was to consist of two parts, a High Court of Justice and a Court of Appeal. In the High Court were to be consolidated all the existing superior courts of first instance. Each of the three Courts of Common Law was to become a division of the High Court, and ultimately all were to be merged in the Queen's Bench Division. The Court of Chancery was to form another division; the Courts of Admiralty, Probate, and Divorce were combined to form a third.

The London Court of Bankruptcy, the Court of
Common Pleas at Lancaster, and the Court of Pleas
at Durham were also merged in the High Court.
The Court of Appeal was to take the place of the
Court of Exchequer Chamber and of the Lords
Justices of Appeal in Chancery, and also (as origin-
ally contrived) of the House of Lords and the Judicial
Committee of the Privy Council.

By the Appellate Jurisdiction Act of 1876, the
former jurisdiction of the House of Lords and of
the Judicial Committee has been maintained, with the
Court of Appeal as an intermediate tribunal between
the High Court and the House of Lords.

Now that the Common Pleas Division and the
Exchequer Division have ceased to exist, the distribution of judges is as follows.   The Queen's Bench
Division consists of fourteen puisne judges, with the
Lord Chief Justice as President.   The Chancery
Division consists of the Lord Chancellor, as President, and five puisne judges.   The Admiralty, Probate, and Divorce Division contains two judges, of
whom one is styled President.   The Court of Appeal
consists of the Master of the Rolls, who no longer
acts as a judge of the first instance, five Lords Justices of Appeal, and the presidents of the several
divisions of the High Court.

The House of Lords as a court of appeal was remodelled by the Act of 1876.   It now includes,

besides the Chancellor and the persons formerly known as the law lords, four Lords of Appeal in Ordinary. These are appointed by the Crown under the provisions of the Act. They must have practised at the Bar for fifteen years, or must have been judges in one or other of the superior courts. They receive a salary of £6000 a year. They are only life peers, but they have all the rights of other peers, even after they have retired from their office. For the purpose of hearing causes three members of the House form a quorum.

Alterations in Procedure. The second object of the Judicature Act of 1873 was the reform of procedure. Details of procedure were left to the judges, who were empowered to make rules of court, which if not called in question in Parliament within a fixed time acquire the force of law. In the main the new procedure was to be a combination of all that was best in Common Law procedure and Equity procedure.

In the Courts of Common Law trial by jury was the invariable rule. Trial by jury was not known in the Court of Chancery. The employment of a jury in the Chancery Division or in the Queen's Bench Division is now largely a matter of convenience and the choice of the parties. In the Common Law Courts a question of law was decided by all the judges. In the Court of Chancery one judge was competent to decide any point of law, and this rule has been adopted in our modern procedure. In the Courts of Common Law evidence was given orally; in the Court of Chancery it was given on affidavit. The modern procedure in both divisions prefers oral evidence, but admits evidence on affidavit when it is the best that can be obtained. A rule of the Common Law (abrogated, however, long before the Judicature Act) forbade a party to a suit to give evidence.[1] In the Court of Chancery evidence was often extracted from the defendant. At the present day the parties may be witnesses in either Division. Repeated attempts have been made to abridge pleadings and to expedite judgment; but the cost and

[1] This rule was abrogated by Lord Denman's Act of 1843 (6 & 7 Vict., c. 85) except in respect to the parties of the record, or persons on whose behalf the proceedings were taken or defended, and their husbands and wives. In 1846 by the Act establishing County Courts, parties, with specified exceptions, were allowed to give evidence in these inferior courts and in 1851 Lord Brougham's Act (14 & 15 Vict., c. 99) made the parties competent witnesses in civil proceedings in the Superior Courts. By the Act of 1853 (16 & 17 Vict., c. 83) husbands and wives of the parties were declared to be admissible witnesses except in two classes of cases which continued subject to the old rule till 1869 (32 & 33 Vict., c. 83). See *Century of Law Reform*, 234-5.

The first statute of this kind in America, admitting testimony of all persons on equal terms, leaving it for the triers to give it, in each case, such weight as it may deserve, was enacted in Connecticut in 1848. This statute appears to have influenced Parliament in passing a similar measure (14 & 15 Vict., c. 99) in 1851. See Baldwin, S. E., *Modern Political Institutions*, 249, n.

For history of rule of common law that interest disqualifies a witness, see *Greenleaf on Evidence*, 16th ed., 487-503.

delay of civil proceedings are still grievous, and the extreme facility of carrying an appeal from court to court is a serious defect in our modern procedure.

The Judicial Committee of the Privy Council. Before quitting the subject of the superior courts, something must be said respecting the Judicial Committee of the Privy Council. The jurisdiction of the superior courts hitherto considered did not comprise ecclesiastical causes, appeals from the Court of Admiralty or from prize courts, or appeals from courts in our colonies or foreign possessions. Appeals from the Ecclesiastical Courts were heard by the Court of Delegates. The members of this court were appointed by royal commission under an Act of Henry VIII. Appeals from the Court of Admiralty were made to the same tribunal. The Privy Council heard appeals from the prize courts and from colonial courts.

An Act of 1832 transferred to the Privy Council the jurisdiction of the Court of Delegates. But the Privy Council had long been unsuited to discharge the function of a court of justice. It was a large body, chiefly composed of persons without legal knowledge. Its legal members would naturally do its legal business, but no such division of labour had yet been enforced by law. What is known as the Judicial Committee of the Privy Council was first established by an Act of 1833. Under this Act the

Judicial Committee was to consist of the Lord
Chancellor and other persons holding high judicial
office, together with two members specially appointed.
Under a later Act the Queen was authorized to
appoint four paid members of the Judicial Committee
who must either at the time of their appointment
or at some previous time have been judges of a
superior court either in England or in India. As the
persons thus appointed die or retire their places will
be filled, under the Act of 1876, by the Lords of
Appeal in Ordinary. For all practical purposes the
Judicial Committee consists of the paid members.
The procedure of the committee bears traces of its
origin from the Privy Council. Its judgments are
couched in the form of advice unanimously given to
her Majesty. The Judicial Committee sits in Downing Street. No other court recorded in history has
had so wide a jurisdiction, or has had to administer
so many different systems of law.

The County Courts. The inferior courts for civil
causes are known as the County Courts. These must
be carefully distinguished from the county courts
of mediæval history. Owing to the small size of the
kingdom, the early predominance of the central
government, and the system of circuits, the ancient
local courts throughout England fell early into decay.
In the beginning of this century there was practically
no provision for the local administration of justice in

civil causes. The only exceptions were such courts
as the Lord Mayor's Court in the City of London, or
the Court of the Hundred of Salford.

With the growth of business and population the
inconvenience became intolerable. Lord Brougham
proposed the establishment of a system of local
courts; but it was only in 1846 that the present
county courts were established.[1] For this purpose
the kingdom has been divided into a number of
districts. Each district corresponding with a Poor
Law union has a county court of its own, and the
style of County Court is therefore misleading. The
districts are grouped into circuits, and all the courts
in a circuit are held by the same judge. In all there
are fifty-nine circuits, but a few are at present without a judge. The County Court Judge is appointed,
and can be removed, by the Lord Chancellor. He
must be a barrister of at least seven years' standing.
His salary is paid by the State, and he may not sit
in the House of Commons. He is assisted by a
registrar, who is always a solicitor by profession, and
who can act for the judge in undefended causes.

The jurisdiction of the county courts extends to all
cases of contract where the sum claimed does not
exceed £50, and to most cases of civil injury where the

[1] For description of events leading to establishment of the modern
County Courts, Lord Cottenham's Act of 1846 and its subsequent
amendment, see W. Blake Odgers in *Century of Law Reform*, 231-4.

damages claimed do not exceed that amount. A variety of other legal business has gradually been transferred to them, but their chief concern is with the recovery of petty debts. As regards procedure a jury is not necessary unless the sum in dispute exceed £5, and either party demand one. The jury consists of five persons. A party may appear either in person or by his solicitor, or he may employ a barrister. Upon points of law there is an appeal to the High Court if the judge gives leave, or as a matter of right if the sum claimed exceeds £20. An appeal from a county court is sometimes carried to the House of Lords. But hundreds of thousands of petty causes are rapidly and cheaply decided by the county courts.

Criminal Procedure. The administration of justice in criminal cases is still based upon the ancient system of circuits, and most of the work is done by the Justices of Assize. But the extraordinary growth of London in the last century led to the erection in 1834 of a permanent court for the trial of indictable offences committed in the capital and the adjoining parts of Kent, Middlesex, and Surrey. This is known as the Central Criminal Court.

The Central Criminal Court.[1] The Lord Mayor, the Lord Chancellor, all the judges of the High Court,

[1] For account of this "greatest criminal court in the world," see 6 State Trials, N. S., 1135.

the Aldermen of the City, and certain other dignified persons are judges of this court. In practice everything is done by judges belonging to the Queen's Bench Division. In extent of jurisdiction and in procedure the Central Criminal Court almost exactly resembles the Assize Courts.

Quarter Sessions. Below the Central Criminal Court and the Courts of Assize come the Courts of Quarter Sessions in the counties and the largest boroughs. In the counties the Court of Quarter Sessions is still composed of all the justices of the peace. To the justices nominated in the traditional way must now be added the chairmen, for the time being, of the County Council and of the district councils within the county. The Quarter Sessions of the large boroughs are held by a Recorder, who must be a barrister of at least five years' standing. In the last century almost all the graver indictable offences were transferred from the jurisdiction of Quarter Sessions to the jurisdiction of the superior courts. Petty offences are still tried by the justices in town and country. A single justice may not inflict a fine of more than 20s., or imprisonment for more than fourteen days. The summary jurisdiction is therefore exercised in most cases by two or more justices in Petty Sessions.

Police Cases. The Crown, however, is authorized by statute to appoint stipendiary magistrates in

London, in municipal boroughs, and in any town of
more than 25,000 inhabitants; and the stipendiary
magistrate, who is always a professional lawyer, has
all the powers of the Petty Sessional Court. The
summary jurisdiction has been remodelled by the
Acts of 1848 and 1879, and under the latter Act
the Petty Sessions have certain powers of trying indictable offences. Thus any indictable offence committed by a child under twelve years of age, other
than homicide, may be summarily dealt with if the
parent or guardian consent. Any accusation in the
nature of larceny or embezzlement against a person
under sixteen years may be summarily dealt with if
the accused gives consent. So may an accusation of
this kind against an adult if the value of the property
in question does not exceed 40s. Lastly, an adult
who pleads guilty to a charge of larceny or embezzlement, even where the value exceeds 40s., may be
summarily dealt with if he has not previously committed an indictable offence. The heaviest penalty
which can be inflicted by a court of summary jurisdiction is a fine of £25 or six months' imprisonment
with hard labour. If an offender is imprisoned
without the option of a fine, he has an appeal to
Quarter Sessions. If he wishes to raise a point of
law he may ask the Petty Sessions to state a case for
the High Court, and if the Petty Sessions refuse, he
may move the High Court for an order requiring a

case to be stated.   Owing to the enlargement of the summary jurisdiction a great number of charges for indictable offences never go to the Quarter Sessions or the Assizes.   And since the Petty Sessions are narrowly restricted in their power of inflicting punishment, there results an indirect mitigation of the severity of the criminal law.

Changes in Criminal Procedure.   Something may here be said regarding the improvement of criminal procedure in the course of this period.[1]   In 1836 prisoners, who had previously been allowed the help of counsel for other purposes, were allowed to employ counsel to make their defence, and were thus placed upon an equality with their prosecutors.   The requirement of an oath on the Gospels to be taken by witnesses has been so modified that persons of any or of no religion may give evidence with a clear conscience, and with full liability to the pains and penalties of perjury.[2]   The perverse rules which forbade an accused person, or the husband or wife of an accused person, to give evidence have been broken through in certain cases,[3] and will probably

[1] For changes in the law of criminal procedure to prevent failure of justice on technical points, see Sir H. B. Poland in *Century of Law Reform*, 60–3.

[2] These changes were made by the Acts of 1833, 1837, and 1869. See W. Blake Odgers in *Century of Law Reform*, 236.

[3] "The Evidence Acts of 1851, 1853 (Brougham's Acts), and of 1869, rendering parties to suits and their husbands and wives competent witnesses, did not apply to criminal cases.   From 1872 to 1897

be abrogated altogether.   Jurors are no longer
denied food or fuel in order to famish them into
unanimity.[1]   A Director of Public Prosecutions has
been created to take care that justice is not defeated
for want of a private person to prosecute; but he has
not hitherto been of much service to the public.

Criminal Appeals.   Another improvement in the
administration of criminal justice was made by the
Act establishing the Court for Crown Cases Reserved.
Subject to certain qualifications, too technical to be
explained here, it may be said that English law does
not confer any right of appeal against the sentence
of a criminal court.   But an Act of 1848 empowers
the judge or the justices in Quarter Sessions to reserve
any point of law for the opinion of a court consisting
of at least five judges now belonging to the Queen's
Bench Division, of whom one must be the Lord Chief
Justice.   The prosecutor or the person convicted
may appear and argue his case, either in person or

---

about twenty-six Acts were passed enabling accused persons in
certain cases to give evidence; but at last came Lord Halsbury's
important Act of 1898 which made an accused person and the
husband and wife of such person *competent* witnesses, and which
regulated the procedure as to their examination."—Sir H. B. Poland,
in *Century of Law Reform*, 53-4. See also Jenks, *Short Hist. of Eng.
Law*, 343-4.

[1] "Under the Juries Act of 1870 the judge may allow the jury at
any time the use of a fire, and they may, at their own expense, have
reasonable refreshment, so that Pope's lines are no longer applicable:
'The hungry judges soon the sentence sign
And wretches hang that jurymen may dine.'"
Sir H. B. Poland in *Century of Law.Reform*, 51.

12

by counsel, and judgment must be given in open
court. The court has the amplest power to reverse,
amend, or affirm any judgment given in the court
below. It is not strictly a Court of Appeal, but rather
a court to determine doubts as to the law entertained
by the judges who hear criminal causes. So well
settled is the criminal law that such doubt is rarely
possible, not twenty cases in a year, according to Sir
James Stephen, coming before the court.[1]

[No provision was made for an appeal from the
finding of a jury on a question of fact until 1907.
The provision then made for such appeal is thus
described by Jenks: "The most striking evidence of
the sensitiveness of the public conscience in the
administration of the criminal law was the establishment, in the year 1907, of the Court of Criminal
Appeal, consisting of the Lord Chief Justice and
eight King's Bench Judges, of whom three, or any
greater uneven number, constitute a quorum. Under
the statute establishing this tribunal, any prisoner,
convicted on indictment, may, with the leave, either
of the tribunal itself or the Court which tried him,
appeal on grounds of fact, or mixed law and fact, or
any other ground, against his conviction; while, with
the leave of the appellate tribunal, he may even
appeal against the amount of his sentence, unless
that is fixed by law. The Court of Criminal Appeal,

[1] See Stephen, *Hist. of Crim. Law of Eng.*, I., 311-13.

on the hearing of an appeal, may totally quash the conviction, or alter the sentence (not necessarily in the appellant's favour); but, if it thinks the appellant was rightly convicted, it is not bound to decide in his favour on a technical point, and, even though the appellant succeeds in upsetting the conviction on one charge in an indictment, or in showing that he has been found guilty of an offence which he did not commit, he may yet be made to serve a proportionate sentence in respect of a charge on which he was properly found guilty, and be sentenced as for conviction on the offence which he really did commit. The Court of Criminal Appeal has, however, no power to direct a new trial. The statute affects neither the prerogative of mercy nor the former right of the accused to appeal on a point of law. But, in the event of the latter being exercised, the appeal will be heard by the new tribunal, which has taken over the duties of the old Court for Crown Cases Reserved."]—*Short Hist. of Eng. Law*, 344–5.

Chief Departments of Law Reform. The progress of reform in substantive law has especially affected the Law of Property, the Law of Contract, and the Law of Corporations. The law of real property, "the Herculaneum of feudalism," being the most archaic part of the law, has undergone the most extensive alteration.

Land Laws. Many attempts have been made to

facilitate the buying and selling of land. Thus the Prescription Act of 1832 has virtually abolished the curious doctrine of time immemorial, and has made it possible to acquire profits and easements (*e. g.*, rights of common or rights of way) by peaceable enjoyment for comparatively brief periods. The Statutes of 1833 and 1874 for the limitation of actions relating to realty have not only curtailed the time within which the owner may sue a stranger in possession, but have deprived him of his title altogether unless he sues within that time. The Fines and Recoveries Act of 1833 has substituted a simple disentailing assurance for the clumsy collusive actions formerly necessary to bar an entail (*i. e.*, to convert an estate tail into an estate in fee simple). The Acts for the Amendment of the Law of Real Property have simplified the methods of conveying land, and the Conveyancing Acts of 1881 and subsequent years have done much to abridge the necessary legal documents.

Another series of Acts culminating in the Settled Land Act of 1882 has enabled the limited owner, whether tenant in tail or tenant for life, to convey to the purchaser of his land an estate in fee simple, and has annulled by anticipation every contrivance for depriving him of this power. These Acts have rendered useless all the expedients formerly employed to keep land in the possession of one family for an indefinite period. Land is still made the subject of settlements, but a settlement now assures to the posterity of the tenant for life not the land, but only a certain amount of wealth, whether invested in land or in certain securities.

In spite of all these reforms, the trouble and expense of proving a title are often considerable, and form an appreciable obstacle to free dealing in land. The complete removal of this obstacle can be effected only by a good system of registration. Two of our greatest lawyers have tried unsuccessfully to establish such a system. Lord Westbury carried an Act for that purpose in 1862, and Lord Cairns carried, in 1875, an Act to remodel Lord Westbury's registry. The machinery for registration of title still exists, but has never been got to work.

Other Acts have provided for the enfranchisement of copyholds, for the commutation of tithe, and for the extinction of the troublesome right of dower. Land has been made fully liable for the debts of a deceased owner, and the heir or devisee of a mortgaged estate can no longer claim that the mortgage debt shall be paid out of the personalty of his predecessor. The law of mortmain and charitable uses has been recently revised and consolidated. The Settled Land Act of 1882 has enabled a tenant for life to grant agricultural, building, or mining leases for long terms. It has also enabled him to expend money derived from the sale of part of the settled land in executing certain permanent improvements upon the land which he retains. The Agricultural Holdings Act of 1883 has secured to the tenant of agricultural land the value of permanent improvements which he has executed. The Allotments Act, 1887, and the Small Holdings Act, 1892, have given the labourer facilities for cultivating land on his own account. The enclosure of commons has been regulated not merely in the interest of those who have rights in the common land, but to provide for the healthy recreation of the general public.

Law of Contract. The Law of Contract has gained in importance through the vast increase of business transactions in the last century.   In this field, however, more has been done to codify existing law than to introduce new principles.   Thus the Bills of Exchange Act, 1882,[1] comprises the entire law of negotiable instruments.   The law of partnership was codified in an Act of 1890,[2] and the law relating to the sale of goods in an Act of 1893.[3]   The Judica-

[1] For history of this Act and Sale of Goods Act, 1893, see "Codification of Mercantile Law," by M. D. Chalmers, *Law Quar. Rev.*, Jan., 1903.

[2] See Introduction to his draft of this Act in *Digest of the Law of Partnership* by Sir Frederick Pollock, St. Louis, F. H. Thomas & Co., 1878.

[3] Of these three Acts, Bills of Exchange and Negotiable Instruments, Partnership Act, and Sale of Goods Act, Pollock says: "So far these codifying measures have worked quite smoothly and have

ture Act of 1873 has facilitated the transfer of rights
arising under a contract. The Infants' Relief Act of
1874 has rendered contracts by persons under age
for goods supplied other than necessaries or for money
lent absolutely void, whereas at Common Law they
were only voidable. The Married Women's Property
Act of 1882 has vastly enlarged the contractual
capacity of married women.[1]

[The Married Women's Property Act, 1882, as
amended in 1893 (56 & 57 Vict., c. 63) is thus
described by Jenks: "That statute not merely
makes all the property of a woman married after
31st December, 1882, and the property of a woman
previously married accruing to her after that date,
her separate property; but it completely emancipates
her from her mediæval incapacities with regard to
alienation and contract, and gives her all legal
remedies for the protection of her rights. It is true,
that her contractual and tortious liabilities can only
be enforced against her to the extent of her separate
estate; and only to that extent in so far as such estate

---

given rise practically to no litigation; that is to say, the cases decided
on their construction have been very few and of those almost all have
been on questions of principle which the Acts had left open because
the existing law left them open, and which would equally have
called for a decision in a jurisdiction where no such statute existed."
—*First Book of Juris.* (1896), 340.

[1] For history of changes in the law affecting the rights, status, and
liabilities of married women, see Montague Lush, *Century of Law
Reform*, ch. xi., also Jenks, *Short Hist. of Eng. Law*, 222–26 and 306.

is not 'restrained from anticipation,' in manner previously explained. But her personal capacity is complete; and a narrow construction which restricted it to cases in which she had separate estate at the time of incurring the liability has been definitely overruled by an amending statute. On the other hand, her husband still remains liable, to the extent of property which he may have acquired through her, for his wife's ante-nuptial liabilities (contractual and tortious); and his mediæval liability for the torts of his wife committed during marriage has not been removed by the Acts. Apparently, however, his former personal liability for her ante-nuptial torts is abolished by the express provisions on that subject of the principal Act. As for a husband's liability for his wife's contracts entered into during marriage, that stands where it did, viz., on the footing of agency. And so a tradesman who in fact gives credit to the husband or the wife may find himself unable to recover from either."]—*Short Hist. of Eng. Law*, 306–7.

Special forms for particular classes of contracts have been imposed by various statutes. Exceptional pains have been taken to render the promoters of companies liable for misrepresentation of fact to persons taking shares. Notwithstanding all these statutes the law of contract remains for the most part case-law.

The Law of Corporations has been enlarged chiefly by the enormous growth of company law. The State has always reserved to itself the power of creating corporate bodies.

Company Law. For a long time this power was exercised either through an Act of Parliament or through royal charter or letters patent, and in either case the instrument creating the corporate body defined its character and organization. This procedure may have sufficed so long as commerce and industry were carried on chiefly by private individuals, and trading corporations like the East India Company or the Bank of England were exceptional; but when commerce and industry, outgrowing individual resources, came to be more and more carried on by joint stock companies, it was necessary to devise a simple and uniform procedure for their creation, and to enact full and precise rules for their government. Companies invested with exceptional powers, such as railway companies, still require an Act of Parliament for their creation, though even here certain general provisions have been enacted once for all (*e. g.*, in the Lands Clauses Consolidation Acts), and applied by reference in the Acts creating particular companies. The law determining the rights and duties of railway companies alone would already fill many volumes. As regards ordinary trading companies the Companies Acts from 1862 onwards have provided for their easy creation and for the conduct of their business. The reported cases which elucidate these Acts may be counted by thousands.[1]

Shipping. In the principal maritime country of the world shipping has naturally attracted the attention of the legislature. The law of ships was consolidated in the Merchant Shipping Act of 1854, now repealed, and again in the Merchant Shipping Act of 1894, the longest and most elaborate Act on the Statute Book.[2]

Labour Legislation. The relations of employer and employed in almost every branch of industry—in mines, in factories, in workshops, and on board ship—have been regulated over and over again in a multitude of Acts. But the liability of the employer for injuries sustained by the workman in the course of his service has not been settled by a permanent Act.

[After reviewing the course of legislation respecting artisan and labour organizations during the last century, Jenks says: "In concluding this long and somewhat painful story, it is pleasant to refer to the beneficent provisions of the Workmen's Compensa-

[1] For the history of Joint Stock and Limited Liability Companies including the Companies Act of 1900 see T. B. Napier, in *Century of Law Reform*, ch. xii.

[2] This Act fills 292 pages in the Law Reports Edition of the Statutes, and in the interval, since 1894, frequently has been amended.

tion Acts 1897, 1900, and 1906, which have enabled a
workman who has suffered injury in the course of his
employment, or the dependents of a workman who
has been killed in such course, to recover compensation from his employers by arbitration proceedings
in the County Court quite apart from any question
of negligence by employer or fellow-workman.
Doubtless these statutes have given rise to much
litigation; and doubtless they are sometimes abused.
But the general adoption of the system of insurance
against liability had practically deprived the measures of all terrors for ordinarily prudent employers;
while the same system has guaranteed compensation
to thousands of deserving workmen who would
otherwise have been dependent upon charity. Bare
allusion may also be made to the Old Age Pensions
Act, 1908, and the Insurance Act, 1911, which will,
in the future, still further alleviate the hardships of
the poorer class of the community."]—*Short Hist.
of Eng. Law*, 330–31.

READINGS

On Common Law and Statute Law, their Rivalry, and the Divergence of Parliamentary and Judicial Law-Making:
Ilbert, *Legislative Methods and Forms*, ch. i.; Dicey, *Law and Opinion in Eng.*, Lecture ii.

On Stages in the Improvement of English Statute Law and Consolidation of Statutes:
Ilbert, *Legislative Methods and Forms*, chaps. iv. and vii.

On Codification:
Jeremy Bentham, *A General View of a Complete Code of Laws*, Bowring's ed., III., 157–210; Ilbert, *Legislative Methods and Forms*, ch. viii.; J. F. Stephen, *Hist. of Crim. Law of Eng.*, III., ch. xxxiv.; Pollock, *Digest of the Law of Partnership*, Introduction; Dillon, *The Laws and Juris. of Eng. and Amer.*, Lectures ix. and x., reprinted in *Anglo-Am. Legal Hist.*, I., ch. xv.; Amos, *Science of Law*, ch. xiii.; Carter, J. C., *The Proposed Codification of our Common Law*, 1884, and *Law, Its Origin, Growth, and Function*, 263–315; Field, D. D., *A Short Response to a Long Discourse*, 1884, an Answer to Pamphlet by J. C. Carter; see also Field, D. D., *Speeches, Arguments, and Miscell. Papers*, I., 307–74, and III., 411–22.

On Changes in the Public Law and Administration of Justice in the Nineteenth Century:
Century of Law Reform, chaps. iv. and v.; art. by Lord Bowen, in Ward, T. H., *The Reign of Queen Victoria*, I., 281–329, reprinted in *Anglo-Am. Legal Hist.*, I., ch. xvi.

On Changes in the Courts of Common Law and Equity and their Procedure in the Nineteenth Century:
Century of Law Reform, chaps. vi. and vii.; Veeder, V. V., "Century of Eng. Judicature," *Green Bag*, XIII., XIV. (1901 and 1902), reprinted in *Anglo-Am. Legal Hist.*, I., ch. xx.

On the Judicature Act of 1873 and its Amendments:
  Carter, *Hist. of Eng. Legal Insti.*, ch. xviii.; Holdsworth, *Hist. of Eng. Law*, I., ch. viii.; Jenks, *Short Hist. of Eng. Law*, 364–71.

On Changes in Criminal Law and Procedure in the Nineteenth
    Century:
  Century of Law Reform, ch. ii.; Jenks, *Short Hist. of Eng. Law*, 337–45.

On Changes in the Law of Real Property in the Nineteenth Century:
  Century of Law Reform, chaps. ix. and x., reprinted in *Anglo-Am. Legal Hist.*, III., ch. lxxi.; Pollock, *The Land Laws* (English Citizen series), ch. vii.; Hogg, "Present Complexity of Land Law and its Remedy," *Law Quar. Rev.*, July, 1904, 292; Jenks, *Short Hist. of Eng. Law*, 239–65.

On Changes in the Law of Personal Property in the Nineteenth
    Century:
  Jenks, *Short Hist. of Eng. Law*, ch. xvi., *passim.*

On Changes in the Law of Contract and Tort in the Nineteenth
    Century:
  Jenks, *Short Hist. of Eng. Law*, ch. xvii., *passim.*

On Changes in the Law of England Affecting Labor in the Nineteenth Century:
  Century of Law Reform, ch. viii.; Jevons, *The State and its Relation to Labor* (English Citizen series); Jenks, *Short Hist. of Eng. Law*, 313–31.

On the Relation between Law and Public Opinion in England during
    the Nineteenth Century:
  Dicey, *Law and Opinion in Eng.*, Lectures iv.–viii. inclusive.

APPENDICES

APPENDIX I

THE EARLIEST ANGLO-SAXON LAWS

THE LAWS OF KING ÆTHELBERT, A.D. 600

THESE ARE THE DOOMS WHICH KING ÆTHELBERT
ESTABLISHED IN THE DAYS OF AUGUSTINE

1. The property of God and of the church, twelve-fold; a bishop's property, eleven-fold; a priest's property, nine-fold; a deacon's property, six-fold; a clerk's property, three-fold; "church-frith," two-fold; "m . . . frith," two-fold.

2. If the king calls his "leod" to him, and any one there do them evil, [let him compensate with] a two-fold "bōt," and L. shillings to the king.

3. If the king drink at any one's home, and any there do any "lyswe," let him make two-fold "bōt."

4. If a freeman steal from the king, let him pay nine-fold.

5. If a man slay another in the king's "tūn," let him make "bōt" with L. shillings.

6. If any one slay a freeman, L. shillings to the king, as "drihtin-beah."

7. If the king's "ambiht-smith," or "laad-rinc," slay a man, let him pay a half "leod-geld."

8. The king's "mund-byrd," L. shillings.

9. If a freeman steal from a freeman, let him make

three-fold "bōt"; and let the king have the "wite" and all the chattels.

10.   If a man lie with the king's maiden, let him pay a "bōt" of L. shillings.

11.   If she be a grinding slave, let him pay a "bōt" of XXV. shillings.   The third [class] XII. shillings.

12.   Let the king's "fed-esl" be paid with XX. shillings.

13.   If a man slay another in an "eorl's" "tūn," let make "bōt" with XII. shillings.

14.   If a man lie with an "eorl's" "birele," let him make "bōt" with XII. shillings.

15.   A "ceorl's" "mund-byrd," VI. shillings.

16.   If a man lie with a "ceorl's" "birele," let him make "bōt" with VI. shillings; with a slave of the second [class], L. "scætts"; with one of the third, XXX. "scætts."

17.   If any one be the first to make an inroad into a man's "tūn," let him make "bōt" with VI. shillings; let him who follows, with III. shillings; after, each, a shilling.

18.   If a man furnish weapons to another where there is strife, though no evil be done, let him make "bōt" with VI. shillings.

19.   If "weg-reaf" be done, let him make "bōt" with VI. shillings.

20.   If a man be slain, let him make "bōt" with XX. shillings.

21.   If a man slay another, let him make "bōt" with a half "leod-geld" of C. shillings.

22.   If a man slay another at an open grave, let him pay XX. shillings, and pay the whole "leod" within XL. days.

23.   If the slayer retire from the land, let his kindred pay a half "leod."

24. If any one bind a freeman, let him make "bōt" with xx. shillings.

25. If any one slay a "ceorl's" "hlaf-æta," let him make "bōt" with vi. shillings.

26. If [any one] slay a "læt" of the highest class, let him pay lxxx. shillings; if he slay one of the second, let him pay lx. shillings; of the third, let him pay xl. shillings.

27. If a freeman commit "edor"-breach, let him make "bōt" with vi. shillings.

28. If any one take property from a dwelling, let him pay a three-fold "bōt."

29. If a freeman pass over an "edor," let him make "bōt" with iv. shillings.

30. If a man slay another, let him pay with his own money, and with any sound property whatever.

31. If a freeman lie with a freeman's wife, let him pay for it with his "wer-geld," and provide another wife with his own money, and bring her to the other

32. If any one thrust through the "riht ham-scyld," let him adequately compensate.

33. If there be "feax-fang," let there be l. sceatts for "bōt."

34. If there be an exposure of the bone, let "bōt" be made with iii. shillings.

35. If there be an injury of the bone, let "bōt" be made with iv. shillings.

36. If the outer "hion" be broken, let "bōt" be made with x. shillings.

37. If it be both, let "bōt" be made with xx. shillings.

38. If a shoulder be lamed, let "bōt" be made with xxx. shillings.

39. If an ear be struck off, let "bōt" be made with xii. shillings.

40. If the other ear hear not, let "bōt" be made with xxv. shillings.

41. If an ear be pierced, let "bōt" be made with iii. shillings.

42. If an ear be mutilated, let "bōt" be made with vi. shillings.

43. If an eye be [struck] out, let "bōt" be made with l. shillings.

44. If the mouth or an eye be injured, let "bōt" be made with xii. shillings.

45. If the nose be pierced let "bōt" be made with ix. shillings.

46. If it be one "ala," let "bōt" be made with iii. shillings.

47. If both be pierced, let "bōt" be made with vi. shillings.

48. If the nose be otherwise mutilated, for each let "bōt" be made with vi. shillings.

49. If it be pierced, let "bōt" be made with vi. shillings.

50. Let him who breaks the chin-bone pay for it with xx. shillings.

51. For each of the four front teeth, vi. shillings; for the tooth which stands next to them iv. shillings; for that which stands next to that, iii. shillings; and then afterwards, for each a shilling.

52. If the speech be injured, xii. shillings. If the collar bone be broken, let "bōt" be made with vi. shillings.

53. Let him who stabs [another] through an arm make "bōt" with vi. shillings. If an arm be broken, let him make "bōt" with vi. shillings.

54. If a thumb be struck off, xx. shillings. If a thumb nail be off, let "bōt" be made with iii. shillings. If the shooting (*i.e.* fore) finger be struck off, let "bōt"

be made with VIII. shillings.   If the middle finger be struck off, let "bōt" be made with IV. shillings. If the gold (*i.e.* ring) finger be struck off, let "bōt" be made with VI. shillings. If the little finger be struck off, let "bōt" be made with XI. shillings.

55.   For every nail, a shilling.

56.   For the smallest disfigurement of the face, III. shillings; and for the greater, VI. shillings.

57.   If any one strike another with his fist on the nose, III. shillings.

58.   If there be a bruise, a shilling; if he receive a right hand bruise, let him [the striker] pay a shilling.

59.   If the bruise be black in a part not covered by the clothes, let "bōt" be made with XXX. "scætts."

60.   If it be covered by the clothes, let "bōt" for each be made with XX. "scætts."

61.   If the belly be wounded, let "bōt" be made with XII. shillings; if it be pierced through, let "bōt" be made with XX. shillings.

62.   If any one be "gegemed," let "bōt" be made with XXX. shillings.

63.   If any one be "cear-wund," let "bōt" be made with III. shillings.

64.   If any one destroy [another's] organ of generation, let him pay him with III. "leud-gelds": if he pierce it through let him make "bōt" with VI. shillings; if it is pierced within let him make "bōt" with VI. shillings.

65.   If a thigh be broken, let "bōt" be made with XII. shillings; if the man become halt, then the friends must arbitrate.

66.   If a rib be broken, let "bōt" be made with III. shillings.

67.   If a thigh be pierced through, for each stab VI. shillings; if (the wound be) above an inch, a shilling; for two inches, II.; above three, III. shillings.

68.   If a sinew be wounded, let "bōt" be made with
III. shillings.

69.   If a foot be cut off, let L. shillings be paid.

70.   If a great toe be cut off, let X. shillings be paid.

71.   For each of the other toes, let one half be paid,
like as it is stated for the fingers.

72.   If the nail of a great toe be cut off, XXX. "scætts"
for "bōt"; for each of the others, make "bōt" with X.
"scætts."

73.   If a freewoman "loc-bore" commit any "leswe,"
let her make a "bōt" of XXX. shillings.

74.   Let "maiden-bōt" be as that of a freeman.

75.   For the "mund" of a widow of the best class,
of an "eorl's" degree, let the "bōt" be L. shillings; of
the second, XX. shillings; of the third, XII. shillings;
of the fourth, VI. shillings.

76.   If a man carry off a widow not in his own tutelage,
let the "mund" be two-fold.

77.   If a man buy a maiden with cattle, let the bargain
stand, if it be without guile; but if there be guile, let
him bring her home again, and let his property be
restored to him.

78.   If she bear a live child, let her have half the
property, if the husband die first.

79.   If she wish to go away with her children, let her
have half the property.

80.   If the husband wish to have them, [let her portion be] as one child.

81.   If she bear no child, let her paternal kindred
have the "fioh," and the "morgen-gyfe."

82.   If a man carry a maiden off by force, let him pay
L. shillings to the owner, and afterwards buy [the object
of] his will of the owner.

83.   If she be betrothed to another man in money,
let him make "bōt" with XX. shillings.

84. If she become "gængang," xxxv. shillings;
and xv. shillings to the king.

85. If a man lie with an "esne's" wife, her husband
still living, let him make two-fold "bōt."

86. If one "esne" slay another unoffending, let him
pay for him at his full worth.

87. If an "esne's" eye and foot be struck out or off,
let him be paid for at his full worth.

88. If any one bind another's "esne," let him make
"bōt" with vi. shillings.

89. Let the "weg-reaf" of a "theow" be iii. shillings.

90. If a "theow" steal, let him make two-fold "bōt."

APPENDIX II

EFFECTS OF THE NORMAN CONQUEST ON THE HISTORY OF ENGLISH LAW AND ON THE DEVELOPMENT OF THE COMMON LAW

[Extracts from *Law and Politics in the Middle Ages*, by Edward Jenks, M.A., 32–44.]

At the time of the Norman Conquest, England is, from a legal standpoint, the most backward of all Teutonic countries, save only Scandinavia. . . . Evidently, English law was, even at the beginning of the twelfth century in a very rudimentary state.

But the Norman Conquest soon changed all this. The Normans were the most brilliant men of their age; and their star was then at its zenith. As soldiers, as ecclesiastics, as administrators, above all, as jurists, they had no equals, at least north of the Alps. . . . The law and the administration of Normandy in the eleventh and twelfth centuries are models for the rest of France. Wherever the Norman goes, to England, to Sicily, to Jerusalem, he is the foremost man of his time. . . .

But the greatest genius will do little unless he is favoured by circumstances; and circumstances favoured the Normans in England. The more rudimentary the English law, the more plastic to the hand of the reformer. . . .

We have now to note the effect of the Norman Conquest on the history of Law.

Law is made local and common.   In the first place, it converted the law of England into a *lex terrae*, a true local law.   There is to be no longer a law of the Mercians, another of the West Saxons, and another of the Danes, not even a law for the English and a law for the Normans, but a law of the land.   It took about a century to accomplish this result, which we doubtless owe to feudal principles.   England was one great fief in the hands of the king, and it was to have but one law.   Writing in the reign of Henry II., Glanville can speak of the "law and custom of the realm."   Such a phrase would then have been meaningless in the mouth of a French or German jurist.   About this time a celebrated expression makes its appearance in England.   Men begin to speak of the "Common Law."   The phrase is not new; but its application is suggestive.   Canonists have used it in speaking of the general law of the Church, as distinguished from the local customs of particular churches.   We may trace it back even to the Theodosian Code.   In the wording of a Scottish statute of the sixteenth century (and this is very suggestive), it will mean the Roman Law.   But, in the mouth of an English jurist of the thirteenth century, it means one thing very specially, viz. the law of the royal court.   And because the royal court is very powerful in England, because it has very little seigneurial justice to fight against, because the old popular courts are already antiquated, the law of the royal court rapidly becomes the one law common to all the realm, the law which swallows up all, or nearly all, the petty local and tribal peculiarities of which the English law, at the time of the Conquest, is full.   The Common Law is the *jus et consuetudo regni* with a fuller development of meaning.   It is not only territorial; it is

supreme and universal.   This is the first great result of
the Conquest. . . .

Law is made judicial.   Again, the Common Law is the
law of a court.   When the Normans first settled in England, they endeavoured to collect law, somewhat in the old
way of the *Leges Barbarorum*, through the wise men of the
shires and the inquests of the king's officials.   At least,
that was long the tradition; and whether or no the *Leges
Eadwardi* which have come down to us are the result of such a process, we may be pretty sure that the
Norman kings made some effort to ascertain what really
were the provisions of those laws and customs of the
English, which they more than once promised to observe.
But these were too formless and too antiquated to suffice
for the needs of an expanding generation.   The whole
work of legal administration had to be put on a different
footing.

This result is achieved in the twelfth century by the
two Henries.   Henry I. (1100–35) begins the practice of
sending his ministers round the country to hear cases in
the local courts.   This is a momentous fact in the history
of English law; but it will be observed that it is not
legislation at all, merely an administrative act. . . .
This practice of provincial visitation withstood the
shock of Stephen's reign; under the great king, who is
both Norman and Angevin (Henry II.), the English
Circuit system struck its roots deep into the soil.
Before the end of the twelfth century, the king's court
has become the most powerful institution in the kingdom, a highly organized body of trained officials, who
make regular visitations of the counties, but who
have a headquarters by the side of the king himself.
This court is at first financial, administrative, judicial.
In course of time the judicial element consolidates
itself; it becomes professional.   It devises regular

forms of proceeding; the first extant Register of Writs
dates from 1227, but, doubtless, earlier registers have
existed for some time in the archives of the Court.
Above all, it keeps a strict and unassailable record of all
the cases which come before it. Any doubt as to precedent can be set at rest by a reference to the Plea Rolls,
which certainly begin before the close of the twelfth
century. Later on, it publishes its proceedings in a
popular form; the first Year Book comes from 1292.
Between the accession of Henry I. (1100) and the death
of Henry III. (1272), this Court has declared the Common
Law of England. That law is to be found, not in cus-
tumals, nor in statutes, nor even in text-books; but in
the forms of writs, and in the rolls of the King's Court.
It is judiciary law; the men who declared it were judges,
not legislators, nor wise men of the shires. No one
empowered them to declare law; but it will go hard
with the men who break the law which they have
declared. . . .

Law is made royal. The Norman Conquest had
strengthened the position of the Crown in England in more
ways than one. . . . Without insisting on the military side
of the Norman Conquest, we may notice the fact that
the kingship of England was, in the hands of William
and his successors emphatically a "conquest," not a
heritage or an elective office. And, when we come to
look at the ideas which have gone to make up our notion
of property, we shall find the *nouveau acquêt*, the "conquest," is much more at the disposal of its master than
the heritage or the office. The Norman Duke who
acquired England made good use of that idea. He
maintained an elaborate pretence of heirship to Edward
the Confessor; but all men must have seen it was a
solemn farce. As Duke of Normandy, he owed at least
nominal allegiance to the King of the French; as King

of England he was "absolute." All was his to give away; what he had not expressly given away, belonged without question to him. Among the documents of the Anglo-Norman period, the *charter* plays a prominent part; and a learned jurist has explained that the essential feature of a charter is that it is a "dispositive" document, a document which transfers to B some right or interest which at present belongs to A. So we get the long and important series of English charters, which culminates in the Great Charter of John and the Merchant Charter of Edward I. When the English Justinian is making his great enquiry into the franchises, which his barons claim to exercise, he insists, and nearly succeeds in maintaining, that, for every assertion of seigneurial privilege, the claimant shall show a royal charter. . . .

But the lord of a domain may make rules for its management, at least with the concurrence of his managing officials. . . . And so it is quite natural to find, in the England of Anglo-Norman times, Assizes and Ordinances which come nearer to modern ideas of law than anything we have seen yet in our search. The Assizes of Clarendon and Northampton, the Assize of Arms, the Woodstock Assize of the Forest, the Assize of Measures in 1197, the Assize of Money in 1205, all these look as though royal legislation is going to take the place of all other law. If Henry of Anjou had been succeeded by one as able as himself, with the magnificent machinery of the royal court to back him, and with no great feudatories to hold him in check, England might very well have come to take her law from the mouth of the king alone. But, fortunately for England, Henry's three successors were not men of his stamp. Richard was able, but frivolous; John, able, but so untrustworthy, that his servants turned against him; Henry, weak and incapable. The danger of royal absolutism passed away. There was even danger that the power of legislation would pass away too, for not only had the royal authority fallen into weak hands, but the king's judges seemed to have lost their inventive power, and the list of writs was almost closed when the third Henry died. Henceforth judicial legislation would proceed only by the slow steps of decision and precedent. . . .

Law is made national. But there arises a king who, consciously or unconsciously, by genius or good luck, is destined to be famous for all time as the propounder of the great idea which is to crown the work of England in the history of Law. Law has been declared by kings, by landowners, by folks, by judges, by merchants, by ecclesiastics. If we put all these forces together, we shall get a law which will be infinitely stronger, better, juster, above all, more comprehensive, than the separate laws which have preceded it. "That which touches all, shall be discussed by all." How far Edward foresaw this result, how far he desired it, how far he borrowed the ideas of others, how far he acted willingly, must be left for specialists to decide. But the broad fact remains, that he created the most effective law-declaring machine in the Teutonic world of his day, that he gave to England her unique place in the history of Law.

APPENDIX III

EXTRACTS FROM MAGNA CARTA[1]

ADMINISTRATION OF LAW AND JUSTICE

Common Pleas. 17. Common pleas shall not follow the King's court, but be held in some certain place.

Assizes. 18, 19. The recognitions of *Novel disseisin*, *Mort d'ancestor*, and *Darrein presentment* shall only be held in the court of the county where the lands in question lie. The King, or in his absence the Chief Justice, shall send two justices into each county four times a year, who, with four knights to be chosen by the county court, shall hold such assizes. If all the matters cannot be determined on the day appointed for each county, a sufficient number of knights and freeholders present at the assizes shall stay to decide them.

Amercements. 20. A freeman shall only be amerced, for a small offence after the manner of the offence, for a great crime according to the heinousness of it, saving to him his contenement; and, after the same manner, a

---

[1] For the Latin text of Magna Carta, see Stubbs's *Select Charters*, 296–306, 2d ed., 1874. For historical explanation and comment upon the following extracts from Magna Carta, see Stubbs's *Consti. Hist. of Eng.*, Vol. I., 533–8; Taswell-Langmead, *Eng. Consti. Hist.*, chap. iv., under text of Magna Carta, *passim;* and McKechnie's *Magna Carta*, part v., chaps. xii., xiv., xvii., xviii., xix., xx., xxi., xxii., xxiv., xxxiv., xxxvi., xxxviii., xxxix., xl., xlii.

merchant saving his merchandise, and a villein saving his wainage; the amercements in all cases to be assessed by the oath of honest men of the neighbourhood.

21. Earls and barons shall not be amerced but by their peers, and according to the degree of the offence.

22. No clerk shall be amerced for his lay tenement except according to the proportions aforesaid, and not according to the value of his ecclesiastical benefice.

Pleas of the Crown. 24. No sheriff, constable, coroner, or bailiff of the King shall hold pleas of the Crown.

Writ of Præcipe in capite. 34. The writ called Præcipe shall not in future be issued so as to cause a freeman to lose his court.

Writ de odio et atia. 36. The writ of inquest of life or limb shall be given *gratis*, and not denied.

Wager of Law. 38. No bailiff for the future shall put anyone to his law (*ad legem*) upon his own bare saying, without credible witnesses to prove it.

" Ne exeat regno " Restrained. 42. In future anyone may leave the kingdom and return at will, unless in time of war, when he may be restrained "for some short space for the common good of the kingdom." Prisoners, outlaws, and alien enemies are excepted, and foreign merchants shall be dealt with as provided in the 41st clause.

FUNDAMENTAL PRINCIPLES OF THE CONSTITUTION

No Scutage or Extraordinary Aid to be Imposed except by the Common Council of the Nation. 12. No scutage or aid shall be imposed unless *per commune concilium regni*, except in the three cases of ransoming the King's person, making his eldest son a knight, and once for marrying his eldest daughter; and for these the aids shall be reasonable. In like manner it shall be concerning the aids of the city of London.

Method of Summons to the National Council. 14. In order to take the common counsel of the Nation in the imposition of aids (other than the three regular feudal aids) and of scutage, the King shall cause to be summoned the archbishops, bishops, earls, and greater barons, by writ directed to each severally, and all other tenants *in capite* by a general writ addressed to the sheriff of each shire; a certain day and place shall be named for their meeting, of which forty days' notice shall be given; in all letters of summons the cause of summons shall be specified; and the consent of those present on the appointed day shall bind those who, though summoned, shall not have attended.

Judicium parium. 39. NO FREEMAN SHALL BE TAKEN OR IMPRISONED OR DISSEISED, OR OUTLAWED, OR EXILED, OR ANYWAYS DESTROYED; NOR WILL WE GO UPON HIM, NOR WILL WE SEND UPON HIM, UNLESS BY THE LAWFUL JUDGMENT OF HIS PEERS, OR BY THE LAW OF THE LAND.

No Sale, Denial, or Delay of Justice. 40. TO NONE WILL WE SELL, TO NONE WILL WE DENY OR DELAY, RIGHT, OR JUSTICE.

APPENDIX IV

THE COMMON LAW — WHAT IT IS, ITS EXPRESSION, AND WHERE IT IS TO BE FOUND

THE COMMON LAW

[From Blackstone, *Commentaries*, I., 67–9.]

THIS unwritten or common law is properly distinguishable into three kinds: 1. General customs; which are the universal rule of the whole kingdom, and form the common law, in its stricter and more usual signification. 2. Particular customs; which, for the most part, affect only the inhabitants of particular districts. 3. Certain particular laws; which, by custom, are adopted and used by some particular courts, of pretty general and extensive jurisdiction.

As to general customs, or the common law properly so called: this is that law, by which proceedings and determinations in the king's ordinary courts of justice are guided and directed. This, for the most part, settles the course by which lands descend by inheritance; the manner and form of acquiring and transferring property; the solemnities and obligation of contracts; the rules of expounding wills, deeds, and acts of parliament; the respective remedies of civil injuries; the several species of temporal offences, with the manner and degree of punishment; and an infinite number of minuter particulars, which diffuse themselves as extensively as the ordinary distribution of common justice requires. Thus, for example, that there shall be four superior courts of record: the Chancery, the King's Bench, the Common Pleas, and the Exchequer; that the eldest son alone is heir to his ancestor; that property may be acquired and transferred by writing; that a deed is of no validity unless sealed and delivered; that wills shall be construed more favourably, and deeds, more strictly; that money lent upon bond is recoverable by action of debt; that breaking the public peace is an offence, and punishable by fine and imprisonment;—all these are doctrines that are not set down in any written statute or ordinance, but depend merely upon immemorial usage, that is, upon common law for their support.

Some have divided the common law into two principal grounds or foundations: 1. Established customs; such as that, where there are three brothers, the eldest brother shall be heir to the second, in exclusion of the youngest; and 2. Established rules and maxims; as, "that the king can do no wrong," "that no man shall be bound to accuse himself," and the like. But I take these to be one and the same thing. For the authority of the maxims rests entirely upon general reception and usage; and the only method of proving that this or that maxim is a rule of the common law is by showing that it hath been always the custom to observe it.

But here a very natural, and very material, question arises; how are these customs or maxims to be known, and by whom is their validity to be determined? The answer is, by the judges in the several courts of justice. They are the depositaries of the laws; the living oracles, who must decide in all cases of doubt, and who are bound by an oath to decide according to the law of the

land. The knowledge of that law is derived from experience and study; from the "*viginti annorum lucubra-
tiones,*" which Fortescue mentions; and from being
long personally accustomed to the judicial decisions
of their predecessors. And, indeed, these judicial
decisions are the principal and most authoritative
evidence that can be given of the existence of such
a custom as shall form a part of the common law.
The judgment itself, and all proceedings previous
thereto, are carefully registered and preserved, under
the name of *records*, in public repositories set apart
for that particular purpose; and to them frequent
recourse is had, when any critical question arises,
in the determination of which former precedents may
give light or assistance.

THE CUSTOM OF THE REALM

[From Sir F. Pollock's *First Book of Jurisprudence*,
240–3.]

There is reason to think, as a matter of history, that in
the critical period when the foundations of English law
were assured, from the reign of Henry II. to that of
Edward I., the king's judges had no small power of determining what customs should prevail and be received as
the "custom of the realm," and that they exercised it
freely. Thus as the end of the twelfth century primo-
geniture does not yet appear as the general law of
inheritance in England, but only as a custom appropriate
to military tenures of land, and occurring indeed in
non-military tenures, but there competing, on equal
terms at best, with equal division among sons or even the
preference of the youngest son. By the end of the
thirteenth century we find it established as the general
rule, and any other order of succession treated as ex-

ceptional. We can hardly resist the inference that it ha
grown by the steady encouragement of the judges. A
the same time there is not much reason to doubt that th
judges fairly represented the effective desires and force
of society at large. . . .

The current description of Common Law as the custon
of the realm is not then to be dismissed as unhistorica]
We have only to remember that the king's judges under
took, from an early time, to know better than the men o
any particular city or country what the custom of th
realm was. Indeed it is plain that local inquiries, i
whatever manner made, could inform them only of loca
usage; and that, so far as general usage really did exis
or tend to exist, the king's judges and officers were th
only persons who had sufficient opportunities of knowin
it; for judicial circuits and personal attendance on th
king in his constant journeys made them familiar, i
the regular course of their duties, with all parts of th
country. More knowledge of England as a whole mus
have been collected at the king's court than could hav
been found anywhere else. Being thus taken charge (
from its birth by a strong centralized power, and d
veloped under the hands of trained professional judg(
and advocates, the Common Law rapidly became
specialized branch of learning worked out by rul(
"scientific" law as the Continental writers say. Muc
of the usage which determined its form was, by th
nature of the case, professional and official usage. Th
methods and practice of the Anglo-Norman chancer
could not have much to do with English custom i
any popular sense. But the *lex et consuetudo reg*
nostri is still there as a whole, and resting on th
same foundation, whatever may be the proportions (
lay and learned, popular and official elements in an
given part of it.

EXPRESSION OF THE COMMON LAW, AND WHERE IT IS TO BE FOUND

[From W. C. Robinson's *Elementary Law*, rev. ed., par. 8, and *Elements of American Jurisprudence*, pars. 227, 232–4.]

The Common Law

The Common Law (called also the unwritten law, or from its mode of development, the customary law) embraces those rules of civil conduct which originated in the common wisdom and experience of society, became in time established customs, and finally received judicial sanction and affirmance in the decisions of the courts of last resort.

Of the Expression of the Common Law

The common or unwritten law is verbally expressed in maxims, definitions, and judicial decisions . . . which are preserved and accessible in the Treatises of jurists and in the Reports of cases. Each of these divisions of our legal literature embraces all the forms of the Unwritten Law. The treatises discuss the decisions of the courts as well as the fixed and fundamental rules of law; the courts in their decisions employ, explain, and affirm the maxims and the definitions. Thus the reports and treatises cannot be distinguished from each other by their subject-matter, but only by its mode of presentation, each mode appropriate to that class of students who find in it the readiest avenue to knowledge. Historically, the appearance of the treatise preceded that of the report. Numerically, the report now outstrips the treatise and forms the major part of all our libraries.

Of the Principal Treatises before the American Revolution

During the century which followed the Norman Conquest legal institutions became settled, courts were established, formal methods of procedure were adopted, the English bench and bar became an influential body in the kingdom, the cultivation of legal learning increased, and the demand for legal treatises inspired private authors to produce them. By order of King Henry II., Ranulph de Glanvill Chief Justiciar of England, composed his famous *Tractatus de Legibus et Consuetudinibus Angliæ* or "Treatise on the Laws and Customs of England." It treats the law from the standpoint of actions for wrongs, in fourteen books, with forms of papers and proceedings. About 1244 Henry Bracton, an LL.D. of Oxford, wrote his *Tractatus de Legibus et Consuetudinibus Angliæ*, a book of great reputation and merit which has been called "the crown and flower of English mediæval jurisprudence." In it the English law is illuminated by an infusion of Roman law, and illustrated by more than five hundred decisions. Two of its five divisions are devoted to personal and property rights; the remaining three to public and private wrongs and remedies. An interval of nearly two centuries then elapsed, during which the foregoing treatises (with a few inferior compends known as Fleta, Britton, and the Mirrour of Justices) and the cases published in the Year Books seem to have met the requirements of the legal profession and the courts, although the law itself steadily developed in scope and precision. At length, in 1471, Sir John Fortescue, the Chief Justice of King's Bench and Lord Chancellor of England, wrote the treatise *De Laudibus Legum Angliæ*, or "Of the Praises of the Laws of England," in which he sets before the future sovereign the excellencies of the common law of England as compared with that of Rome and other countries. It is our first book on Comparative Jurisprudence and seems to have been intended as an introduction to a larger work on the whole body of the law which never was completed. Littleton's *Tenures*, a treatise on the law of Real Property and the foundation of the works of Coke and Blackstone, written by Thomas de Littleton, a judge of the Common Pleas and the most distinguished lawyer of the reign of Edward IV., was printed in 1481. It soon became the text-book of all students of the law, and the statements and definitions of its author were accepted as of the same authority as a judgment of the courts. Under the reign of Henry VIII. the principal law-writer was Anthony Fitzherbert, also a judge of the Court of Common Pleas. His first work, published in 1514, was a *Grand Abridgment of the Law*, a work of "singular learning and utility." His second and most famous one was the *Natura Brevium*, or "Nature of Writs," printed in 1534, a treatise on the different writs by which actions could be commenced and the grounds on which they should be issued. It is a discussion of the law from the point of view of wrongs and remedies, and was a book of very high authority. In the same reign appeared the *Register of Writs* printed in 1531, a collection of the authorized forms of writs. These forms were very early settled by the courts, and the matter in this Register is the oldest formulated matter in our law. It contains writs adapted to every species of legal wrong and to every step in judicial procedure. Great learning was expended in framing these writs. They were regarded as "the measure of legal rights" and the Register itself as a manual of the greatest authority. The period of seventy-eight years between the reign of Henry VIII. and that of Charles I. witnesses many changes in the social and political conditions of the Eng-

lish people and many corresponding alterations in the
law, forerunners of the disappearance of the Norman
feudal system under Cromwell and the second Charles,
and the substitution of the sovereignty of commerce for
that of arms.   The connecting link between the older
legal institutions and the new is the *Institutes* by Sir
Edward Coke, a work which is the foundation of the
literature of our modern law.   Lord Coke was born in
1551, and died in 1634.   He was law lecturer of the
Inner Temple and Chief Justice, first of Common Pleas
and afterwards of King's Bench.   His *Institutes* were
published in 1628.   The First Institute is a Commentary on Littleton's *Tenures*.   The Second treats of
the Statutes from Magna Charta till the reign of Henry
VIII., with explanations drawn from the decisions of the
Courts.   The Third is on the Pleas of the Crown, or
Criminal Law.   The Fourth discusses the Jurisdiction of
the Courts.   Coke's *Institutes* still occupy a high position
among the treatises on English law, especially the First
Institute, which has been often published as a separate
work by various editors with copious notes and explanations.   Sir Matthew Hale, a judge of Cromwell's
reign in 1653, produced, among a variety of works, a
History of the Law and an *Analysis of the Civil Part of our
Law*.   The latter seems to have been intended as a
refutation of the critics of the common law who complained that it was not a rational science "by reason of
the indigestiveness of it and the multiplicity of the cases
in it."   This analysis supplied Sir William Blackstone
with the plan of his *Commentaries*, and was probably the
first attempt to give a logical harmony and sequence to
the Unwritten Law.   One hundred years afterwards,
in 1753, Blackstone, at the age of thirty, began his
lectures at Oxford on the common law, which were published under the name of Blackstone's **Commentaries**

between 1765 and 1769. These *Commentaries* reproduce, explain, and supplement the works of Hale, Coke, Bracton, and Glanvill and all other previous writers on the English law. Appearing on the eve of our Revolution they represent the laws of England as they stood when the separation of the American colonies from the mother country made them sovereign states, and when they adopted as their own so much of that law as they deemed suitable to their condition. Blackstone thus contains the English portion of our law, of course with much beside that is not law for us, and therefore always has been and always must be a treatise of great practical importance to the American Bar.

Of the Principal Reports before the American Revolution

The Year Books contain the earliest published reports of the judicial decisions of the English courts. They were commenced by royal authority in 1324 under the reign of Edward II., and continued without interruption for about two hundred years, when in the reign of Henry VIII. through motives of false economy they were suspended. Private commercial enterprise or literary ambition then assumed the task, and until the reign of Queen Victoria carried it forward with varying success.[1] The names of the collectors and publishers of cases decided in the courts of common law and equity during these three centuries constitute a formidable array, among them being judges of the highest eminence who thus preserved their own decisions, and their work was sometimes well and sometimes ill performed. The

[1] Since 1865 the reports of cases decided in the English Courts have been issued under the supervision of a Council of Law Reporting, a body which represents the Inns of Court and the General Council of the Bar.

principal common law reporters before and during the epoch of the Revolution were Dyer (1513–1582), Plowden (1550–1580), Coke (1572–1616), Hobart (1603–1625), Croke (1582–1641), Yelverton (1603–1613), Saunders (1666–1673), Vaughan (1665–1674), T. Jones (1667–1685), Levinz (1660–1697), Palmer (1619–1629), Pollexfen (1669–1685), W. Jones (1620–1641), Lord Raymond (1694–1734), Salkeld (1689–1712), Strange (1716–1749), Comyns (1695–1741), Willes (1737–1760), Wilson (1742–1774), Burrow (1757–1771), Cowper (1774–1778), Douglass (1778–1784), Durnford and East (1785–1800), East (1801–1812), Henry Blackstone (1788–1796), William Blackstone (1746–1780), Bosanquet and Puller (1796–1807). The reported decisions of the courts of equity for the same period are found in Chancery Cases (1557–1606), Dickens (1559–1798), Vernon (1681–1720), Precedents in Chancery (1689–1723), Peere Williams (1695–1736), Mosely (1726–1731), Talbot (1734–1738), Vesey and Atkins (1747–1756), Ambler (1737–1784), Eden (1757–1767), Brown (1778–1794), Cox (1783–1796), Vesey 2d (1789–1796). The cases in these Reports are of authority in the United States on such rules of the English law as have become incorporated into our own.

APPENDIX V

EQUITY—WHAT IT IS; ORIGIN AND DEVELOP-MENT OF COURTS OF EQUITY

[Extract from W. C. Robinson's *Elementary Law*, rev. ed., 385–6, par. 348.]

EQUITY signifies equality or justice, and when the word is used in general works on jurisprudence it is sometimes defined as "the correction of that wherein the law, by reason of its universality, is deficient." In the system of the Common Law, however, it denotes certain remedial processes by which relief can be afforded in cases whose peculiar circumstances place them beyond the reach of the ordinary courts.

Of the Origin and Development of Courts of Equity

The *courts of common law*, adhering to their ancient customs and refusing to take jurisdiction over causes for which no precedent existed, left five classes of private legal controversies entirely without redress. These were: (1) Cases requiring a preventive remedy; (2) Cases involving more than two antagonistic parties; (3) Cases to which the customary forms of common law actions were not adapted; (4) Cases in which a judgment for damages, or for the restoration of specific property, afforded no adequate relief; (5) Cases in which the defendant had a just defence but under the current rules of pleading and procedure was unable to present it. In these cases the sole resort of the suitor was to the king in person, who by his chancellor investigated and decided the controversy; thus gradually establishing *a new tribunal* side by side with the courts of common law, but with practically unlimited jurisdiction and able to apply its remedies to every species of private injury. Until the reign of Richard II. (A.D. 1377–99), the authority of this tribunal was chiefly spiritual; but at that time it began to issue *writs of subpœna*, summoning the parties into court as witnesses, and then detaining them until they complied with its decrees. By this means it obtained control over the persons of the parties, and became able to enforce its orders under penalty of perpetual imprisonment. During the next two centuries the growing power of this tribunal aroused the apprehensions of the courts of common law, and its authority was often called in question; but in the reign of James I. (A.D. 1616) the king himself set these matters at rest by deciding that the chancellor could grant relief even against the judgment of a court of common law.[1] Since that date equity jurisdiction has rapidly expanded. In this country it is sometimes vested in the courts of common law, sometimes in distinct judicial bodies. Under the *New Procedure* both systems are combined, and legal and equitable remedies may be sought and applied in the same action.

[1] See page 124 and note.

APPENDIX VI

THE ENGLISH STATUTE BOOK

[Extracts from *Legislative Methods and Forms*, by Sir Courtenay Ilbert, K.C.S.I., chap. ii., 20–34.]

WHAT is the English Statute Book? What are its contents? Where are they to be found? How are they arranged? What facilities are there for ascertaining the enactments which have been made on a given subject, and the extent to which they are in force?

The object of this chapter is to supply an answer to these questions.

Meaning of "Statute"

The word "Statute" is in ordinary English usage treated as equivalent to Act of Parliament, and the English Statute Book might therefore be expected to include all Acts passed by the Parliament of England, or, since the union with Scotland and Ireland respectively, by the Parliament of the United Kingdom. But the Statute Book includes certain enactments which are not, in the strictest sense, Acts of Parliament, and excludes certain enactments which are. When Parliament was first taking shape as a legislative body, laws were made, not by the King, Lords, and Commons in Parliament assembled, but by the king, with the counsel and assent of the great

men of the realm, and the legislation of the reign of
Henry III. and most of that of Edward I. was the work
of assemblies to which the Commons were not summoned.
The line between Royal Ordinances and Acts of Parliament is not easy to draw in the first stages of Parliamentary legislation, and some of the most important among
the early enactments in the English Statute Book, including the Statute "Quia Emptores," would not comply with the tests applied to a modern Act of Parliament.
On the other hand, the ordinary editions of the "Statutes
at Large" exclude numerous Acts of Parliament as being
either local or private. The line between general and
local, public and private, Acts has been drawn variously
at different times, and will be referred to hereafter. For
the present, the Statute Book will be treated as including
only the public general Statutes.

Statutes of the Realm

The first edition of the English Statutes which was
at once authoritative and collective was that commonly
known as the *Statutes of the Realm*. . . . This edition
. . . including every law, as well those repealed or
expired, as those now in force, with a chronological list
of them, and tables of their principal matters, was
prepared by the first Record Commissioners, pursuant
to a report of a Committee of the House of Commons of
July 4, 1800, and an address to the Crown, and was
entitled *Statutes of the Realm, printed by command of His
Majesty King George III., in pursuance of an address
from the House of Commons of Great Britain, from
original records and authentic manuscripts*. This edition
is in nine folio volumes, of which the first was published
in 1810, and the last in 1822, and contains the Statutes
from Henry III.'s Provisions of Merton (1235–6) to the

last year of the reign of Queen Anne (1713). Prefixed to
these Statutes, in the first volume, are prints of certain
" charters of liberties, " including Magna Charta, and an
elaborate introduction, which, though superseded on
some points by later researches, contains a large amount
of interesting and valuable information on the history
and condition of the English Statute Law. . . . The
edition was supplemented by two index volumes.

Scottish Statutes

In pursuance of a resolution passed by the Record
Commission in 1807, a folio edition of the Scottish
Statutes was prepared on lines resembling the English
edition of the *Statutes of the Realm.* In order to give
further time for consideration of the difficulties connected
with the earlier Statutes, it was arranged that the first
volume should be postponed. Accordingly, vols. II. to
XI., containing the Statutes from 1424 to 1707, the date
of the union with England, were brought out in the years
1814 to 1824, whilst the first volume, containing documents of earlier date, did not appear until 1844. . . .
A revised edition of the Ante-Union Scottish Statutes is
in course of preparation.

Irish Statutes

The Record Commission did not bring out any edition
of the Irish Statutes, but a revised edition of the Ante-
Union Irish Statutes from 1710 to 1800, comprised in
a single quarto volume, was brought out under the
authority of the Irish Government in 1888.

Editions of Statutes at Large for Period Since 1713

For the period since the reign of Queen Anne no collective edition of the English Statutes, containing repealed

as well as unrepealed matter, has been published by authority. Of the editions brought out by private enterprise in the eighteenth century, the most important were those by Serjeant Hawkins (1734–5) and by Mr. Ruffhead (1762–4). These editions were regularly continued by subsequent volumes, and as they were printed from the King's Printers' copies of the Statutes, their contents for the period since 1707 may be relied on as accurate; but they omit Statutes which are treated as of minor or transitory importance. King's Printers' copies of the nineteenth century Statutes have been published in many forms, and an octavo edition of the Acts of each session is now published by the Stationery Office within a reasonable time after the end of the session.

Chitty's " Statutes of Practical Utility"

The edition most commonly used by practising lawyers is Chitty's *Statutes of Practical Utility*. In this edition all the Statutes which the profession are considered likely to want are printed with short notes, and are grouped under subjects which are alphabetically arranged. The latest edition, by W. H. Aggs, is in fifteen octavo volumes, and is brought down to the end of 1911. Two supplementary volumes extended to March, 1913.

Revised Statutes

The object of the Statute Law Revision Acts which have been passed from 1861 onwards has been to purge away dead matter from the Statute Book, and thus to facilitate the preparation of an edition of the Statutes which should contain only such acts as are in force.

The latest edition of such Revised Statutes known as Statutes Revised, second edition (1235–1886), was published in sixteen octavo volumes, 1888–1900.

Appendix V

Annual Volumes of Public General Statutes

The year 1886 was selected as the termination of the period for the Revised Statutes, because the existing edition of the Annual Statutes begins with the following year. Down to the year 1887 the Annual Statutes were printed and published in different forms and at different prices. From the beginning of 1887, one authoritative edition only of the Statutes is published annually, in an octavo volume, at a cheaper price than formerly, and is edited by an officer paid by the Treasury. Each volume contains an index to the public general Acts of the session to which it relates.

INDEX

227